A Concordance to the *Collected Poems* of JAMES JOYCE

Edited by

Paul A. Doyle

Nassau Community College

State University of New York

The Scarecrow Press, Inc.

New York & London 1966

L. C. Card No. 66-13738

In Memory of

Ann Keating Doyle (1926-1963)

whose one shilling copy of

Pomes Penyeach

started this project

Preface

Chamber Music (1907), Pomes Penyeach (1927), and Ecce Puer (1932) form James Joyce's Collected Poems. The Black Sun Press first issued this compilation in December, 1936. In 1937 the Viking Press published this edition, eventually adding two earlier published broadsides - The Holy Office (1904) and Gas from a Burner (1912) - and made all of this verse conveniently available in the Portable James Joyce (1947). The hard cover editions of Joyce's Collected Poems have long been out of print, but Viking published a paperback edition in 1957, which has gone through several printings, and, of course, the Portable James Joyce continues to be highly popular.

It is the purpose of this concordance not only to serve as a reference tool by enabling general readers to locate immediately passages of particular interest, but also to furnish students and scholars with the opportunity to study Joyce's poetic imagery more closely, to reflect on the richness and beauty of his word choice, and to correlate various uses of the same word.

A not uncommon graduate school seminar pastime a few decades ago was the study of Alexander Pope's verse imagery in order to furnish data for the debate about whether his word usage made him a member of the school of neoclassicism or a forerunner of pre-romanticism. Several readers will recall the value of Edwin Abbott's concordance to Pope on such occasions and will at once understand how a concordance helps to increase immeasurably both appreciation and a more complete understanding of an author's work. This aspect is especially important in analyzing the writings of James Joyce since he is the great modern master of words in all their variety - both in impact and connotation. It is hoped that this present book will render the study of Joyce's imagery in his published poems a more facile and organized task.

This concordance is a word index to the Collected Poems - including, of course, the two selections found in the

Portable James Joyce - and gives the various words, the line or lines of verse in which the word appears, the title of the poem, and the line number. (For those readers not too familiar with Joyce's poetry, it should be recalled that the poems in the *Chamber Music* volume are untitled. They are designated by Roman numerals from I to XXXVI.)

Almost all of Joyce's uncollected poetry is too casual and too ephemeral in composition and in nature to be of special significance. Much of this verse was written in personal letters and consists of jingles, parodies, and doggerel. Further, much of Joyce's miscellaneous poetry exists only in fragments. (A descriptive catalogue of Joyce's miscellaneous poems compiled by the present editor may be found in the Winter 1965 number of the *James Joyce Quarterly.*) It is on the beauty of *Ecce Puer*, the lovely lyrics in the *Chamber Music* group, and several of the *Penyeach* poems that Joyce's reputation as a poet will rest. This concordance, therefore, treats of the poems which Joyce himself wished to have before the public eye and leave for posterity.

This present volume follows the standard concordance practice of not indexing certain common and frequently recurring articles, conjunctions, and prepositions. The following words have not been indexed: a, an, and, at, by, for, from, in, of, on, the, to, with. Where necessary, catchtitles are adopted. The list of abbreviated headings used for the full titles includes the following poems:

	Poems
Watching	Watching the Needleboats at San Sabba
A Flower	A Flower Given to My Daughter
She Weeps	She Weeps over Rahoon
Tutto	Tutto è Sciolto
On the Beach	On the Beach at Fontana
A Memory	A Memory of the Players in a Mirror at Midnight
Gas	Gas from a Burner

This concordance is a concrete example of the chain reaction of literary interest and enthusiasm. My wife, the late Ann Keating Doyle, became a devotee of Joyce's writing while taking courses at Columbia University Graduate School under the eminent Joycean, William York Tindall. She, in turn, passed on an interest in Joyce to me, and this book owes its basic impetus to her.

P. A. Doyle

Nassau Community College
State University of New York

A Concordance to the Collected Poems of

JAMES JOYCE

abed

Or him who once when snug abed
The Holy Office 43

about

Whose song about my heart is falling?
IV 10

Sad songs about the end of love;
XXVIII 2

Sing about the long deep sleep
XXVIII 5

And the thunder of horses plunging, foam about their knees:
XXXVI 2

Talk about Irish Names of Places!
Gas 60

above

Soft sweet music in the air above
III 14

He drives his beasts above Cabra.
Tilly 4

Loveward above the glancing oar
Watching 2

Darkness of fear above
On the Beach 10

Vast wings above the lambent waters brood
Flood 3

Who soars above on an angel's wing
Gas 46

accounted

But I must not accounted be
The Holy Office 23

ache

Ache of love!
On the Beach 12

act
I act as vicar-general
The Holy Office 60

adequate
To adequate the balance-sheet.
The Holy Office 90

adieu
Bid adieu, adieu, adieu,
XI 1
Bid adieu to girlish days,
XI 2

admonisheth
Whose leaves the morn admonisheth.
XV 4

adoring
Voidward from the adoring
Nightpiece 17

adorning
With springtide all adorning her?
VIII 2

Aeschylus
The long-lost works of Aeschylus.
The Holy Office 46

afar
I moan in sleep when I hear afar their whirling laughter.
XXXVI 6

afraid
For Love at first is all afraid.
XXX 4

after
That will not after,
X 6
He travels after a winter sun,
Tilly 1
But weeping after holy fast
The Holy Office 35

again
Your hand again.
XVII 4
Sweetheart, be at peace again -
XIX 3
Highhearted youth comes not again
Bahnhofstrasse 6
Again!
A Prayer 1
Again!
A Prayer 13

aglow
Whose way in heaven is aglow
III 12

ago
He sent me a book ten years ago:
Gas 5

Ah
Ah, could they ever hold me there
XXII 5
Ah star of evil! star of pain!
Bahnhofstrasse 5

air
Strings in the earth and air
I 1
The old piano plays an air,
II 5
Soft sweet music in the air above
III 14
A merry air.
V 4
A merry air,
V 14
In silvery arches spanning the air,
IX 5
With many a pretty air.
XXIV 4
Under a pretty air,
XXIV 12
All fair, with many a pretty air
XXIV 15
Till the irreverent mountain air
XXV 5

air (continued)
Dusk of the air.
Tutto 8
And, gathering, she sings an air:
Simples 7
I flash my antlers on the air.
The Holy Office 88
My penitent buttocks to the air
Gas 92

alarms
That night allures me where alarms
XXII 9

Alas
Alas! Why will you use me so?
XXIX 12

all
All softly playing,
I 9
At that hour when all things have repose,
III 1
When all things repose do you alone
III 6
All maidenly, disconsolate,
IV 2
Austerities were all the sweeter
VI 9
With springtide all adorning her?
VIII 2
The ways of all the woodland
VIII 9
For whom does all the sunny woodland
VIII 11
All you that love.
X 4
Go seek her out all courteously,
XIII 1
Making to tremble all those veils
XV 7
Be not sad because all men
XIX 1
They are sadder than all tears;
XIX 5
My hope and all my riches is,
XXIII 2

My hope and all my riches - yes! -
XXIII 5
And all my happiness.
XXIII 6
All fair, with many a pretty air
XXIV 15
Ripple all thy flying hair.
XXV 6
And all for some strange name he read
XXVI 11
Dearest, my lips wax all too wise;
XXVII 8
In the grave all love shall sleep:
XXVIII 7
For Love at first is all afraid.
XXX 4
Rain has fallen all the day.
XXXII 1
And all around our loneliness
XXXIII 9
The leaves - they do not sigh at all
XXXIII 11
All day I hear the noise of waters
XXXV 1
All day, all night, I hear them flowing
XXXV 11
Was all but thine?
Tutto 12
All night a veil,
Alone 2
And all my soul is a delight,
Alone 7
Come, give, yield all your strength to me!
A Prayer 2
Or him who sober all the day
The Holy Office 29
Confesses all his pagan past -
The Holy Office 36
But show to all that poor - dressed be
The Holy Office 39
But all these men of whom I speak
The Holy Office 47
To sister mummers one and all
The Holy Office 59
I printed it all to the very last word
Gas 9

allow
(Allow me, ladies, to blow my nose)
Gas 28

allures
That night allures me where alarms
XXII 9

alone
When all things repose do you alone
III 6
Forth alone,
XXXV 4
My love, my love, my love, why have you left me alone?
XXXVI 12
Unfellowed, friendless and alone,
The Holy Office 85

along
There's music along the river
I 5
Along with us the summer wind
XXXI 5
Urging the cattle along a cold red road,
Tilly 2

always
This lovely land that always sent
Gas 15

am
'Tis I that am your visitant.
IV 12
Believe me rather that am wise
XII 7
Come! I yield. Bend deeper upon me! I am here.
A Prayer 16

amend
Can make amend -
XVII 6

amethyst
The twilight turns from amethyst
II 1
With lights of amethyst.
II 12

amid
Hear you amid the drowsy even
IV 3
Who goes amid the green wood
VIII 1
Who goes amid the merry green wood
VIII 3

among
Among the apple-trees,
VII 2
Among his foes in scorn and wrath
XXI 3
O come along the laden trees:
XXXII 2

ancient
Of Love in ancient plenilune,
XII 3
Holding to ancient nobleness,
XXI 4

angel's
Who soars above on an angel's wing
Gas 46

anguish
Subduer, do not leave me! Only joy, only anguish,
A Prayer 17

answer
Proudly answer to their tears:
XIX 7

answering
And the night wind answering in antiphon
III 9

answers
That answers my corruptive "would."
The Holy Office 66

antiphon
And the night wind answering in antiphon
III 9

antique
For elegant and antique phrase,
XXVII 7

antlers
I flash my antlers on the air.
The Holy Office 88

anvil
Clanging, clanging upon the heart as upon an anvil.
XXXVI 8

any
There is no word nor any sign
XVII 5
Found any soul to fellow his,
XXI 2
She cannot find any more Stuarts to sell.
Gas 68

anything
Grieve not, sweetheart, for anything -
XXXIII 17

anywhere
Saw you my true love anywhere?
IX 6

apart
Unhappy when we draw apart
XXIII 3

apparel
The woods their rich apparel wear -
VIII 14

appear
Where softly-burning fires appear,
XV 6

appease
With him who hies him to appease
The Holy Office 25

apple-trees
Among the apple-trees,
VII 2

Aquinas
Steeled in the school of old Aquinas.
The Holy Office 82

arches

In silvery arches spanning the air,
IX 5

Arches on soaring arches,
Nightpiece 5

are

The odorous winds are weaving
XIV 5

For lo! the trees are full of sighs
XV 3

The flowery bells of morn are stirred
XV 10

They are sadder than all tears;
XIX 5

Lowliest attendants are;
XXV 10

Of lovers that are dead, and how
XXVIII 6

Still you are beautiful - but O,
XXIX 3

The grey winds, the cold winds are blowing
XXXV 7

Frail the white rose and frail are
A Flower 1

Grey way whose violet signals are
Bahnhofstrasse 3

Ladies and gents, you are here assembled
Gas 1

Where Christ and Caesar are hand and glove!
Gas 26

arise

Arise, arise!
XIV 2

Arise, arise,
XIV 7

Arise, arise!
XIV 16

From dewy dreams, my soul, arise,
XV 1

Aristotle

The mind of witty Aristotle,
The Holy Office 6

arm

And boyish arm.
On the Beach 8

armour
Arrogant, in black armour, behind them stand,
XXXVI 3

arms
Dearest, through interwoven arms
XXII 7
Soft arms that woo me to relent
XXII 3

army
I hear an army charging upon the land,
XXXVI 1

around
And all around our loneliness
XXXIII 9
Around us fear, descending
On the Beach 9

arrogant
Arrogant, in black armour, behind them stand,
XXXVI 3

arse
'Twould give you a heartburn on your arse:
Gas 40

arses
Thus I relieve their timid arses,
The Holy Office 55

art
Fair as the wave is, fair, art thou!
Simples 8

artilleryman
With her tight-breeched British artilleryman
Gas 82

artists
Her writers and artists to banishment
Gas 16

arts
Because of the black and sinister arts
Gas 3

as

That wander as they list --
II 10

The young leaves as they pass,
VII 6

As lover to lover,
X 15

Their lives ascend as a continual sigh.
XIX 6

As they deny, deny.
XIX 8

For there, as in some mossy nest
XXIII 7

Shall we not be as wise as they
XXIII 11

That makes as one thing to the lover
XXIV 13

Sad as the sea-bird is, when going
XXXV 3

Clanging, clanging upon the heart as upon an anvil.
XXXVI 8

Then as now.
She Weeps 8

As his sad heart has lain
She Weeps 10

As thou, fond heart, love's time, so faint, so far,
Tutto 3

Falling as through the silence falleth now
Tutto 7

Fair as the wave is, fair, art thou!
Simples 8

Lambent and vast and ruthless as is thine
Flood 11

As the bleak incense surges, cloud on cloud,
Nightpiece 16

As sour as cat's breath,
A Memory 6

The signs that mock me as I go
Bahnhofstrasse 8

Gentling her awe as to a soul predestined.
A Prayer 5

My scarlet leaves them white as wool:
The Holy Office 57

I act as vicar-general
The Holy Office 60

Indifferent as the herring-bone,
The Holy Office 86

as (continued)
Firm as the mountain-ridges where
The Holy Office 87
Let them continue as is meet
The Holy Office 89
Nor make my soul with theirs as one
The Holy Office 93
Though (asking your pardon) as for the verse
Gas 39
In the playboy shift that he pinched as swag
Gas 47
My conscience is fine as Chinese silk:
Gas 69
My heart is as soft as buttermilk.
Gas 70
I'll sing a psalm as I watch it burn
Gas 87

ascend
Their lives ascend as a continual sigh.
XIX 6

ashes
And a little ashes
XVIII 7
And the ashes I'll keep in a one-handled urn.
Gas 88

aside
Lay aside sadness and sing
XXVIII 3

asking
Though (asking your pardon) as for the verse
Gas 39

assail
Desolate winds assail with cries
XXIX 7

assembled
Ladies and gents, you are here assembled
Gas 1

attempt
Lest bards in the attempt should err
The Holy Office 7

attendants
Lowliest attendants are;
XXV 10

attire
My love is in a light attire
VII 1
Carry so brave attire?
VIII 12
My little love in light attire
The Holy Office 71

austerities
Because of sad austerities
VI 4
Austerities were all the sweeter
VI 9

Austrian
That was over here dressed in Austrian yellow,
Gas 50

avenue
The trees of the avenue.
II 4

awake
Awake to hear the sweet harps play
III 7

awaken
The lost hosts awaken
Nightpiece 8

away
Love is unhappy when love is away!
IX 9
Calling us away?
XVI 6
Sweet love, away.
XX 16

awe
Gentling her awe as to a soul predestined.
A Prayer 5

aweary
Love is aweary now.
XXVIII 8

awful
My awful sin I will confess.
Gas 94

backwards
Backwards and forwards, down and up,
Gas 7

bag
From Maunsel's manager's travelling bag.
Gas 48

balance-sheet
To adequate the balance-sheet.
The Holy Office 90

ban
But Mammon places under ban
The Holy Office 73

banishment
Her writers and artists to banishment
Gas 16

bannerets
Vainly your loveblown bannerets mourn!
Watching 6

Bannockburn
My Irish foreman from Bannockburn
Gas 95

bards
Lest bards in the attempt should err
The Holy Office 7

barge
The leaky barge of the Bishop of Rome
Gas 22

bastard
Where they talk of "bastard," "bugger" and "whore,"
Gas 32

bat
When the bat flew from tree to tree
XXXI 2

battle-name
They cry unto the night their battle-name:
XXXVI 5

be
Nor muse: Who may this singer be
IV 9
I would in that sweet bosom be
VI 1
I would in that sweet bosom be.
VI 5
I would be ever in that heart
VI 6
Where only peace might be my part.
VI 8
The foam flies up to be garlanded,
IX 4
No more be tears in moon or mist
XII 11
And soon will your true love be with you,
XIII 15
My breast shall be your bed.
XIV 12
Begin (innumerous!) to be heard.
XV 12
Friends be untrue
XVIII 6
Be not sad because all men
XIX 1
Sweetheart, be at peace again -
XIX 3
But sleep to dreamier sleep be wed
XXII 11
Shall we not be as wise as they
XXIII 11
Neither a love where may not be
XXVII 11
And soon shall love dissolved be
XXIX 9
Be mine, I pray, a waxen ear
Simples 9
Must here be my interpreter:
The Holy Office 8

be (continued)
Be piteous or terrible
The Holy Office 12
How can one fail to be intense?
The Holy Office 22
But I must not accounted be
The Holy Office 23
But show to all that poor-dressed be
The Holy Office 39
Nor can they ever be exempt
The Holy Office 77
Till the Mahamanvantara be done:
The Holy Office 94

bear
In a manner no blackamoor printer could bear.
Gas 54

beasts
He drives his beasts above Cabra.
Tilly 4

beautiful
My dove, my beautiful one,
XIV 1
My dove, my beautiful one!
XIV 8
Still are you beautiful - but O,
XXIX 3

beauty
How is your beauty raimented!
XXIX 4
That shadowy beauty in her eyes,
The Holy Office 64

because
Because of sad austerities
VI 4
Because your voice was at my side
XVII 1
Because within my hand I held
XVII 3
Be not sad because all men
XIX 1
Nor grieve because our love was gay
XXXIII 5

Because of the black and sinister arts
Gas 3

become
The zone that doth become thee fair,
XI 5

bed
My breast shall be your bed.
XIV 12
At night when close in bed she lies
The Holy Office 69

bees
The wild bees hum.
X 12

before
To Love before him on his way,
III 8
Prefer a lying clamour before you:
XIX 2
Before the looking-glass.
XXIV 8
Yet will we kiss, sweetheart, before
XXXIII 15
He drives them with a flowering branch before him,
Tilly 7

begin
Begin thou softly to unzone
XI 9
Begin (innumerous!) to be heard.
XV 12

behind
Arrogant, in black armour, behind them stand,
XXXVI 3

belch
For everyone knows the Pope can't belch
Gas 23

believe
Believe me rather that am wise
XII 7

bells
The flowery bells of morn are stirred
XV 10

bellyful
Through me they purge a bellyful.
The Holy Office 58

beloved
Come, my beloved, where I may
XXXII 7
Blind me with your dark nearness, O have mercy, beloved enemy of my will!
A Prayer 7

below
And in the earth below.
III 15
Clouds that wrap the vales below
XXV 8
Far below.
XXXV 10

bend
O bend no more in revery
IV 7
My slow life! Bend deeper on me, threatening head,
A Prayer 10
Come! I yield. Bend deeper upon me! I am here.
A Prayer 16

bending
My love goes slowly, bending to
VII 7

bends
She bends upon the yellow keys,
II 7

beneath
Glory and stars beneath his feet --
XII 4

bent
With head to the music bent,
I 10

bequeaths
Who a mad tale bequeaths to us
XXVI 9

beside
And sobbing beside my printing press
Gas 93

betrayed
Betrayed her own leaders, one by one.
Gas 18

between
And happy between kiss and kiss;
XXIII 4
And feels my hand between her thighs
The Holy Office 70

bid
Bid adieu, adieu, adieu,
XI 1
Bid adieu to girlish days,
XI 2

Billy
Without the consent of Billy Walsh
Gas 24

birdless
A birdless heaven, seadusk, one lone star
Tutto 1

bishop
The leaky barge of the Bishop of Rome
Gas 22

black
Arrogant, in black armour, behind them stand,
XXXVI 3
I bleed by the black stream
Tilly 11
Under the moongrey nettles, the black mould
She Weeps 11
Because of the black and sinister arts
Gas 3

blackamoor
In a manner no blackamoor printer could bear.
Gas 54

blazes
I'm damned if I do - I'm damned to blazes!
Gas 59

bleak
As the bleak incense surges, cloud on cloud,
Nightpiece 16

bleed
I bleed by the black stream
Tilly 11

blind
Blind me with your near darkness, O have mercy, beloved enemy of my will!
A Prayer 7

blinding
They cleave the gloom of dreams, a blinding flame,
XXXVI 7

bloody
But I draw the line at that bloody fellow
Gas 49

blow
When over us the wild winds blow -
XXIX 10
(Allow me, ladies, to blow my nose)
Gas 28

blowing
Singing: The bridal wind is blowing
XIII 13
The grey winds, the cold winds are blowing
XXXV 7

blue
To deep and deeper blue,
II 2
The twilight turns to darker blue
II 11
And where the sky's a pale blue cup
VII 9

blueveined
My blueveined child.
A Flower 8

bolder
He sings the bolder;
X 10

bond
Boor, bond of the herd,
Tilly 9

bone
Lies not, stark skin and bone.
A Memory 9

book
My book was closed;
V 5
I have left my book,
V 9
He sent me a book ten years ago:
Gas 5
A red-headed Scotchman to keep my book.
Gas 66
I'll burn that book, so help me devil.
Gas 86

books
I printed mystical books in dozens:
Gas 37

boor
Boor, bond of the herd,
Tilly 9

born
A child is born
Ecce Puer 2

bosom
I would in that sweet bosom be
VI 1
VI 5
Thy girlish bosom unto him
XI 10

both
Through both the ends of a telescope.
Gas 8

bough
For my torn bough!
Tilly 12

boyish
And boyish arm.
On the Beach 8

brain
From far a low word breathes on the breaking brain
A Prayer 3
From far her low word breathe on my breaking brain.
A Prayer 15

brains
'Tis Irish brains that save from doom
Gas 21

branch
He drives them with a flowering branch before him,
Tilly 7

brave
Carry so brave attire?
VIII 12

breaking
From far a low word breathes on the breaking brain
A Prayer 3
From far her low word breathe on my breaking brain.
A Prayer 15

breast
White breast of the dove,
XIV 11
My breast shall be your bed.
XIV 12
Her smooth round breast;
XVIII 14

breath
But softer than the breath of summer
XXXI 7

Love's breath in you is stale, worded or sung,
A Memory 5
As sour as cat's breath,
A Memory 6

breathe
From far her low word breathe on my breaking brain.
A Prayer 15

breathed
Young life is breathed
Ecce Puer 9

breathes
From far a low word breathes on the breaking brain
A Prayer 3

bridal
Singing: The bridal wind is blowing
XIII 13

bright
Bright cap and streamers,
X 1

bringing
Bringing to tavern and to brothel
The Holy Office 5

British
With her tight-breeched British artilleryman
Gas 82

brood
Vast wings above the lambent waters brood
Flood 3

brooding
Where brooding day stares down upon the sea
Flood 7

brothel
Bringing to tavern and to brothel
The Holy Office 5

brow
The clear young eyes' soft look, the candid brow,
Tutto 5

brow (continued)
And moonlight kisses her young brow
Simples 6

brown
Now, O now, in this brown land
XXXIII 1

brute
They moo and make brute music with their hoofs.
Tilly 6

bugger
Where they talk of "bastard," "bugger and "whore."
Gas 32

bugles
The bugles of the cherubim
XI 8

bum
Memento homo upon my bum.
Gas 98

burn
I'll burn that book, so help me devil.
Gas 86

I'll sing a psalm as I watch it burn
Gas 87

but
A sage that is but kith and kin
XII 5

But one unto him
XVIII 9

But sleep to dreamier sleep be wed
XXII 11

Though love live but a day?
XXIII 12

Is his, if thou but scan it well,
XXVI 8

And I but render and confess
XXVII 5

Still are you beautiful - but O,
XXIX 3

But you, dear love, too dear to me,
XXIX 11

But softer than the breath of summer
XXXI 7
Was all but thine?
Tutto 12
But I must not accounted be
The Holy Office 23
But weeping after holy fast
The Holy Office 35
But show to all that poor-dressed be
The Holy Office 39
But all these men of whom I speak
The Holy Office 47
But Mammon places under ban
The Holy Office 73
But by the mercy of the Lord
Gas 10
But I draw the line at the bloody fellow
Gas 49

buttermilk
My heart is as soft as buttermilk.
Gas 70

buttocks
My penitent buttocks to the air
Gas 92

button
To show you for strictures I don't care a button
Gas 29

Cabra
He drives his beasts above Cabra.
Tilly 4

Caesar
Where Christ and Caesar are hand and glove!
Gas 26

cakeshop
Downes's cakeshop and Williams's jam?
Gas 58

calling
When he at eventide is calling,
IV 8
And hear you not the thrushes calling,
XVI 5

calling (continued)
Calling us away?
XVI 6
Calling to them, a voice they know,
Tilly 3
Sad is his voice that calls me, sadly calling,
She Weeps 3
How soft, how sad his voice is ever calling,
She Weeps 6

calls
Sad is his voice that calls me, sadly calling,
She Weeps 3

calm
Its cruel calm, submission's misery,
A Prayer 4
Calm in his cradle
Ecce Puer 5

came
Love came to us in time gone by
XXX 1

can
Can make amend --
XVII 6
Can they dishonour you?
XIX 4
How can one fail to be intense?
The Holy Office 22
For I can do those things for them
The Holy Office 51
Nor can they ever be exempt
The Holy Office 77
Colm can tell you I made a rebate
Gas 71

candid
The clear young eyes' soft look, the candid brow,
Tutto 5

cannot
She cannot find any more Stuarts to sell.
Gas 68
For everyone knows the Pope can't belch
Gas 23

And some women's legs that I can't recall,
Gas 34

cap
Bright cap and streamers,
X 1

Capuchin
With the comedian Capuchin?
XII 6

care
To show you for strictures I don't care a button
Gas 29

carry
Carry so brave attire?
VIII 12
I carry off their filthy streams
The Holy Office 50

Castilian
His high Castilian courtesy --
The Holy Office 40

catch-as-catch-can
Plays every night at catch-as-catch-can
Gas 81

cat's
As sour as cat's breath,
A Memory 6

cattle
Urging the cattle along a cold red road,
Tilly 2

cease
I pray you, cease to comb out,
XXIV 9
Cease, silent love! My doom!
A Prayer 6

cedar
I wait by the cedar tree,
XIV 9

Celtic
With gold-embroidered Celtic fringes --
The Holy Office 28

chant
Know you by this, the lover's chant,
IV 11

charging
I hear an army charging upon the land,
XXXVI 1

charioteers
Disdaining the reins, with fluttering whips, the charioteers.
XXXVI 4

cherubim
The bugles of the cherubim
XI 8

child
My blueveined child
A Flower 8
In the still garden where a child
Simples 3
A child is born
Ecce Puer 2
A child is sleeping:
Ecce Puer 13

childish
To shield me from her childish croon
Simples 10

Chinese
My conscience is fine as Chinese silk:
Gas 69

choir
For many a choir is singing now
XVI 3

choiring
In that soft choiring of delight
XXVI 3

choirs
And the wise choirs of faery
XV 11

choose
Will choose her what you see to mouth upon.
A Memory 11

Christ
Saw Jesus Christ without his head
The Holy Office 44
Where Christ and Caesar are hand and glove!
Gas 26

church
Those things for which Grandmother Church
The Holy Office 53

clamour
Prefer a lying clamour before you:
XIX 2

clanging
Clanging, clanging upon the heart as upon an anvil.
XXXVI 8

clear
Through the clear mirror of your eyes,
XXIX 5
The clear young eyes' soft look, the candid brow,
Tutto 5

cleave
They cleave the gloom of dreams, a blinding flame,
XXXVI 7

clique
Make me the sewer of their clique.
The Holy Office 48

close
We take sad leave at close of day.
XXXIII 16
At night when close in bed she lies
The Holy Office 69

closed
My book was closed;
V5

cloud
As the bleak incense surges, cloud on cloud,
Nightpiece 16

clouds
Clouds that wrap the vales below
XXV 8

clustered
Your clustered fruits to love's full flood,
Flood 10

clusters
The rockvine clusters lift and sway.
Flood 2

cold
The grey winds, the cold winds are blowing
XXXV 7
Urging the cattle along a cold red road,
Tilly 2
Dark too our hearts, O love, shall lie and cold
She Weeps 9
I dare not withstand the cold touch that I dread.
A Prayer 8

colder
From whining wind and colder
On the Beach 5

Colm
Colm can tell you I made a rebate
Gas 71

comb
I pray you, cease to comb out,
XXIV 9
Comb out your long hair,
XXIV 10

combing
Silently she's combing,
XXIV 1
Combing her long hair,
XXIV 2
And still she's combing her long hair
XXIV 7

come

At that hour when soft lights come and go,
III 13

And he is come to visit you.
IV 6

Come follow, come follow,
X 3

Sweetheart, I come.
X 16

Happy Love is come to woo
XI 3

And say I come,
XIII 2

And come into her little garden
XIII 11

Their words come to.
XVIII 8

Come with me now,
XX 15

Lightly come or lightly go:
XXV 1

O come among the laden trees:
XXXII 2

Come, my beloved, where I may
XXXII 7

They come shaking in triumph their long, green hair:
XXXVI 9

They come out of the sea and run shouting by the shore.
XXXVI 10

Come, give, yield all your strength to me!
A Prayer 2

Come! I yield. Bend deeper upon me! I am here.
A Prayer 16

comedian

With the comedian Capuchin?
XII 6

comes

Highhearted youth comes not again
Bahnhofstrasse 6

Comes to pass.
Ecce Puer 12

common

Ruling one's life by common sense
The Holy Office 21

companies
To run in companies.
VII 4

companion
His love is his companion.
XXI 6

company
One of that mumming company --
The Holy Office 24

conduct
Or him whose conduct "seems to own"
The Holy Office 31

confess
And I but render and confess
XXVII 5
My awful sin I will confess.
Gas 94

confesses
Confesses all his pagan past --
The Holy Office 36

conjurable
At ghosting hour conjurable --
XXVI 10

conscience
My conscience is fine as Chinese silk:
Gas 69

consent
Without the consent of Billy Walsh.
Gas 24

console
While they console him when he whinges
The Holy Office 27

contempt
From his taxation of contempt.
The Holy Office 78

continual
Their lives ascend as a continual sigh.
XIX 6

continue
Let them continue as is meet
The Holy Office 89

cool
O cool is the valley now
XVI 1
O cool and pleasant is the valley
XVI 7
In deep cool shadow
XX 3
Of cool sweet dew and radiance mild
Simples 1

corruptive
That answers my corruptive "would."
The Holy Office 66

could
Ah, could they ever hold me there
XXII 5
In a manner no blackamoor printer could bear.
Gas 54
I wish you could see what tears I weep
Gas 75

counsel
What counsel has the hooded moon
XII 1

countless
On Mammon's countless servitors
The Holy Office 76

country
I love my country -- by herrings I do!
Gas 74

courteously
Go seek her out all courteously,
XIII 1

courtesy
Now, wind, of your good courtesy
XIII 9
His high Castilian courtesy --
The Holy Office 40

Cousins
I printed the table-book of Cousins
Gas 38

cradle
Calm in his cradle
Ecce Puer 5

crawled
Where they have crouched and crawled and prayed
The Holy Office 83

crazy
The crazy pierstakes groan;
On the Beach 2

crew
The shamblings of that motley crew,
The Holy Office 80

cries
Desolate winds assail with cries
XXIX 7

crisscross
And sign crisscross with reverent thumb
Gas 97

croon
To shield me from her childish croon
Simples 10

crouched
Where they have crouched and crawled and prayed
The Holy Office 83

crucifix
Neither to malt nor crucifix
The Holy Office 38

cruel
Its cruel calm, submission's misery,
A Prayer 4

cry
Through the soft cry of kiss to kiss,
XXIX 6

He hears the winds cry to the waters'
XXXV 5
They cry unto the night their battle-name:
XXXVI 5

crying
A voice crying "Sleep now"
XXXIV 3
Is crying "Sleep no more."
XXXIV 8
I heard their young hearts crying
Watching 1

cup
And where the sky's a pale blue cup
VII 9

Curly's
He forgot to mention Curly's Hole.
Gas 62

Curtis
To O'Leary Curtis and John Wyse Power
Gas 52

dainty
Her dress with dainty hand.
VII 12

dames'
His giddy dames' frivolities
The Holy Office 26

damned
I'm damned if I do -- I'm damned to blazes!
Gas 59

dance
Watching the fire dance
V 7
Winds of May, that dance on the sea,
IX 1

dancing
Dancing a ring-around in glee
IX 2

Dante
A Dante is, unprejudiced,
The Holy Office 16

dappled
And on the dappled grass,
XXIV 6

dare
I dare not withstand the cold touch that I dread.
A Prayer 8
The "dare not" of sweet maidenhood
The Holy Office 65

dark
Dark leaves on his hair.
I 8
O, hurry over the dark lands
XIII 5
In the dark pine - wood
XX 1
Where my dark lover lies.
She Weeps 2
Ever unanswered and the dark rain falling,
She Weeps 7
Dark too our hearts, O love, shall lie and cold
She Weeps 9
Blind me with your dark nearness, O have mercy, beloved enemy of my will!
A Prayer 7
Of the dark past
Ecce Puer 1

darker
The twilight turns to darker blue
II 11

darkness
Darkness of fear above
On the Beach 10
The darkness of my mind was rent
Gas 11

dawn
Eastward the gradual dawn prevails
XV 5

day
At noon of day.
XX 4
At noon of day
XX 14
Though love live but a day?
XXIII 12
Rain has fallen all the day.
XXXII 1
We take sad leave at close of day.
XXXIII 16
All day I hear the noise of waters
XXXV 1
All day, all night, I hear them flowing
XXXV 11
Of sullen day.
Flood 4
Where brooding day stares down upon the sea.
Flood 7
Whereto I pass at eve of day,
Bahnhofstrasse 2
Or him who sober all the day
The Holy Office 29

days
Bid adieu to girlish days,
XI 2

dead
Of lovers that are dead, and how
XXVIII 6

dear
Dear lady, a divining ear.
XXVI 2
Dear heart, why will you use me so?
XXIX 1
Dear eyes that gently me upbraid,
XXIX 2
But you, dear love, too dear to me,
XXIX 11
When the dear love she yielded with a sigh
Tutto 11
Or him who loves his Master dear --
The Holy Office 41
And writing of Dublin, dirty and dear,
Gas 53

dearest
My soul, dearest, is fain --
XXII 2
Dearest, through interwoven arms
XXII 7
Dearest, my lips wax all too wise;
XXVII 8

death
From love's deep slumber and from death,
XV 2

deep
To deep and deeper blue,
II 2
From love's deep slumber and from death,
XV 2
In deep cool shadow
XX 3
Sing about the long deep sleep
XXVIII 5
And in my heart how deep unending
On the Beach 11

deeper
To deep and deeper blue
II 2
My slow life! Bend deeper on me, threatening hand,
A Prayer 10
Come! I yield. Bend deeper upon me! I am here.
A Prayer 16

defy
Framed to defy the poison - dart,
XXVII 2

delight
In that soft choiring of delight
XXVI 3
And all my soul is a delight,
Alone 7

deny
As they deny, deny. XIX 8

depart
Of memories shall we depart.
XXXII 6

descending
Thy kiss descending
XX 9
Around us fear, descending
On the Beach 9

deserts
From the grey deserts of the north?
XXVI 6

deserving
The poor and deserving prostitute
Gas 80

desire
Where the gay winds do most desire
VII 3
Knows the soft flame that is desire.
The Holy Office 72

desolate
Desolate winds assail with cries
XXIX 7

despair
My heart, have you no wisdom thus to despair?
XXXVI 11

detail
And woo me to detain.
XXII 4

detect
For I detect without surprise
The Holy Office 63

devil
I'll burn that book, so help me devil.
Gas 86

devour
Pluck and devour!
A Memory 14

dew
His song is softer than the dew
IV 5

dew (continued)

The pale dew lies
XIV 13

Of cool sweet dew and radiance mild
Simples 1

dewy

From dewy dreams, my soul, arise,
XV 1

diadem

Through which I lost my diadem,
The Holy Office 52

did

Where Love did sometime go.
XVI 4

My love and I did walk together;
XXXI 3

Where Love did so sweet music make
XXXIII 2

dim

In moonless gloom each lapses muted, dim,
Nightpiece 10

dip

Shall dip his right hand in the urn
Gas 96

dire

Dire hunger holds his hour.
A Memory 12

dirty

And writing of Dublin, dirty and dear,
Gas 53

disconsolate

All maidenly, disconsolate,
IV 2

disdain

In dull disdain.
Flood 8

disdaining
Disdaining the reins, with fluttering whips, the charioteers.
XXXVI 4

dishevelled
I, who dishevelled ways forsook
The Holy Office 3

dishonour
Can they dishonour you?
XIX 4

disregard
In disregard of the divine,
XII 8

dissolved
And soon shall love dissolved be
XXIX 9

distantly
So distantly I turn to view
The Holy Office 79

divers
The wrens will divers treasures keep,
XXIII 8

divide
For seas and land shall not divide us
XIII 7

divine
In disregard of the divine,
XII 8

divining
Dear lady, a divining ear.
XXVI 2

do
Do you hear the night wind and the sighs
III 3
When all things repose do you alone
III 6
Where the gay winds do most desire
VII 3

do (continued)
Do nothing move.
X 8
Gentle lady, do not sing
XXVIII 1
The leaves -- they do not sigh at all
XXXIII 11
Subduer, do not leave me! Only joy, only anguish,
A Prayer 17
For I can do those things for them
The Holy Office 51
I do a similar kind service
The Holy Office 62
Shite and onions! Do you think I'll print
Gas 55
I'm damned if I do -- I'm damned to blazes!
Gas 59
I love my country -- by herrings I do!
Gas 74
I'll penance do with farts and groans
Gas 89

does
For whom does all the sunny woodland
VIII 11

done
Till the Mahamanvantara be done:
The Holy Office 94

Donnycarney
O, it was out by Donnycarney
XXXI 1

don't
To show you for strictures I don't care a button
Gas 29

doom
Cease, silent love! My doom!
A Prayer 6
'Tis Irish brains that save from doom
Gas 21
Poor sister Scotland! Her doom is fell;
Gas 67

door
Is heard at the door.
XXXIV 6

And though they spurn me from their door
The Holy Office 95

doth
The zone that doth become thee fair,
XI 5

dove
My dove, my beautiful one,
XIV 1
My dove, my beautiful one!
XIV 8
White breast of the dove,
XIV 11
My fair one, my fair dove,
XIV 15

down
Where brooding day stares down upon the sea
Flood 7
Backwards and forwards, down and up,
Gas 7

Downes's
Downes's cakeshop and Williams's jam?
Gas 58

downfall
Proud by my downfall, remembering, pitying
A Prayer 11

dozens
I printed mystical books in dozens:
Gas 37

drab
From the drunken draggletail Dublin drab.
Gas 84

draggletail
From the drunken draggletail Dublin drab.
Gas 84

draw
Unhappy when we draw apart
XXIII 3
Draw from me still
A Prayer 9

draw (continued)
But I draw the line at the bloody fellow
Gas 49

dread
I dare not withstand the cold touch that I dread.
A Prayer 8

dream
That they may dream their dreamy dreams
The Holy Office 49

dreamers
Leave dreams to the dreamers
X 5

dreamier
But sleep to dreamier sleep be wed
XXII 11

dreaming
And the time of dreaming
X 13

dreams
Leave dreams to the dreamers
X 5
Dreams is over --
X 14
From dewy dreams, my soul, arise,
XV 1
They cleave the gloom of dreams, a blinding flame,
XXXVI 7
That they may dream their dreamy dreams
The Holy Office 49

dreamy
That they may dream their dreamy dreams
The Holy Office 49

dress
Her dress with dainty hand
VII 12
A rogue in red and yellow dress
XXXIII 7

dressed
That was over here dressed in Austrian yellow,
Gas 50

drinks
Or him who drinks his pint in fear --
The Holy Office 42

drives
He drives his beasts above Cabra.
Tilly 4
He drives them with a flowering branch before him,
Tilly 7

drowsy
Hear you amid the drowsy even
IV 3

drunken
From the drunken draggletail Dublin drab.
Gas 84

dry
'Twas Irish humour, wet and dry,
Gas 19

Dublin
And writing of Dublin, dirty and dear,
Gas 53
From the drunken draggletail Dublin drab.
Gas 84

dull
In dull disdain.
Flood 8

dusk
Dusk of the air.
Tutto 8

duty
But I owe a duty to Ireland:
Gas 13

each
A senile sea numbers each single
On the Beach 3

each (continued)
In moonless gloom each lapses muted, dim,
Nightpiece 10
And for each maiden, shy and nervous,
The Holy Office 61

ear
Dear lady, a divining ear.
XXVI 2
Be mine, I pray, a waxen ear
Simples 9

earth
Strings in the earth and air
I 1
And in the earth below.
III 15
Together, folded by the night, they lay on earth. I hear
A Prayer 14
To hear why earth and heaven trembled
Gas 2

ease
One positively needs the ease
The Holy Office 13

eastward
Eastward the gradual dawn prevails
XV 5

elegant
For elegant and antique phrase,
XXVII 7

emigrant
When I think of the emigrant train and ship.
Gas 76

enaisled
Enaisled is!
XX 8

end
Sad songs about the end of love;
XXVIII 2

ended
Which now is ended in this way.
XXXIII 6

ends
Through both the ends of a telescope.
Gas 8

enemy
Blind me with your dark nearness, O have mercy, beloved enemy of my will!
A Prayer 7

enough
How love that passes is enough
XXVIII 4

enshrouded
Enshrouded, wave
Nighpiece 3

enter
To enter heaven, travel hell,
The Holy Office 11

entreat
(O soft I knock and soft entreat her!)
VI 7

epithalamium
Epithalamium.
XIII 4

ere
Ere that mine eyes had learned to weep.
XXIII 10

Erin
So gross a libel on Stepmother Erin.
Gas 64

err
Lest bards in the attempt should err
The Holy Office 7

estimate
Of one hundred pounds on the estimate
Gas 72

eve
Whereto I pass at eve of day,
Bahnhofstrasse 2

even
Hear you amid the drowsy even
IV 3

evenstar
At the hour of evenstar
XXV 9

eventide
When he at eventide is calling,
IV 8

ever
I would be ever in that heart
VI 6
So I were ever in that heart.
VI 10
Wind of spices whose song is ever
XIII 3
Ah, could they ever hold me there
XXII 5
Lightly, lightly -- ever so:
XXV 7
Ever so little falsity.
XXVII 12
How soft, how sad his voice is ever calling,
She Weeps 6
Ever unanswered and the dark rain falling,
She Weeps 7
And that high spirit ever wars
The Holy Office 75
Nor can they ever be exempt
The Holy Office 77

evermore
My soul shall spurn them evermore.
The Holy Office 96

every
For every true - born mysticist
The Holy Office 15
Plays every night at catch-as-catch-can
Gas 81

everyone
For everyone knows the Pope can't belch
Gas 23

evil
Ah star of evil! star of pain!
Bahnhofstrasse 5
Who was it said: Resist not evil?
Gas 85

exempt
Nor can they ever be exempt
The Holy Office 77

extremes
Hazards extremes of heterodoxy,
The Holy Office 18

eye
Flung quicklime into Parnell's eye;
Gas 20

eyes
Shy thoughts and grave wide eyes and hands
II 9
A glory kindles in those eyes,
XII 9
Upon my lips and eyes.
XIV 4
Ere that mine eyes had learned to weep.
XXIII 10
Dear eyes that gently me upbraid,
XXIX 2
Through the clear mirror of your eyes,
XXIX 5
In gentle eyes thou veilest,
A Flower 7
The clear young eyes' soft look, the candid brow,
Tutto 5
The eyes that mock me sign the way
Bahnhofstrasse 1
Unclose his eyes!
Ecce Puer 8
That shadowy beauty in her eyes,
The Holy Office 64

faery
And the wise choirs of faery
XV 11

fail
When friends him fail.
XVIII 4

fail (continued)
How can one fail to be intense?
The Holy Office 22

fain
My soul, dearest, is fain --
XXII 2

faint
As thou, fond heart, love's time, so faint, so far,
Tutto 3
Ghostfires from heaven's far verges faint illume,
Nightpiece 4

fair
(O sweet it is and fair it is!)
VI 2
That is so young and fair.
VIII 16
The zone that doth become thee fair,
XI 5
My fair one, my fair dove,
XIV 15
All fair, with many a pretty air
XXIV 15
Rosefrail and fair -- yet frailest
A Flower 5
Fair as the wave is, fair, art thou!
Simples 8

fall
When the year takes them in the fall.
XXXIII 12

fallen
Rain has fallen all the day.
XXXII 1

falleth
Falling as through the silence falleth now
Tutto 7

falling
Whose song about my heart is falling?
IV 10
Rain on Rahoon falls softly, softly falling,
She Weeps 1

Ever unanswered and the dark rain falling
She Weeps 7
Falling as through the silence falleth now
Tutto 7

falls
Rain on Rahoon falls softly, softly falling,
She Weeps 1

falsity
Ever so little falsity.
XXVII 12

far
Far below.
XXXV 10
As thou, fond heart, love's time, so faint, so far,
Tutto 3
Ghostfires from heaven's far verges faint illume,
Nightpiece 4
From far a low word breathes on the breaking brain
A Prayer 3
From far her low word breathe on my breaking brain.
A Prayer 15
That's why I publish far and wide
Gas 77

farts
I'll penance do with farts and groans
Gas 89

fast
But weeping after holy fast
The Holy Office 35

father
O, father forsaken,
Ecce Puer 15

fear
What sound hath made thy heart to fear?
XXVI 4
And one in fear was standing nigh --
XXX 3
Around us fear, descending
On the Beach 9
Darkness of fear above
On the Beach 10

fear (continued)
Or him who drinks his pint in fear --
The Holy Office 42

feels
And feels my hand between her thighs
The Holy Office 70

feet
Glory and stars beneath his feet --
XII 4

fell
Poor sister Scotland! Her doom is fell;
Gas 67

fellow
Found any soul to fellow his,
XXI 2
But I draw the line at the bloody fellow
Gas 49

fills
The lamp fills with a pale green glow
II 3

filthy
I carry off their filthy streams
The Holy Office 50

find
She cannot find any more Stuarts to sell.
Gas 68

finds
Like him who finds a joy at table
The Holy Office 19

fine
My conscience is fine as Chinese silk:
Gas 69

fineboned
And touch his trembling fineboned shoulder
On the Beach 7

fingers
And fingers straying
I 11

fire
   Watching the fire dance
      V 7
   Gleam with a soft and golden fire --
      VIII 10
   Tonight stretch full by the fire!
      Tilly 10

fires
   Where softly - burning fires appear,
      XV 6

firm
   Firm as the mountain - ridges where
      The Holy Office 87

first
   For Love at first is all afraid.
      XXX 4
   O Ireland my first and only love
      Gas 25

flame
   They cleave the gloom of dreams, a blinding flame,
      XXXVI 7
   Knows the soft flame that is desire.
      The Holy Office 72

flash
   I flash my antlers on the air.
      The Holy Office 88

flesh
   Your itch and quailing, nude greed of the flesh,
      A Memory 4

flew
   When the bat flew from tree to tree
      XXXI 2

flies
   The foam flies up to be garlanded,
      IX 4

flood
   Goldbrown upon the sated flood
      Flood 1
   Your clustered fruits to love's full flood,
      Flood 10

floor
On the floor.
V 8

flowering
He drives them with a flowering branch before him,
Tilly 7

flowers
Pale flowers on his mantle,
I 7

flowery
The flowery bells of morn are stirred
XV 10

flowing
All day, all night, I hear them flowing
XXXV 11

flung
Flung quicklime into Parnell's eye;
Gas 20

fluttering
Disdaining the reins, with fluttering whips, the charioteers.
XXXVI 4
This heart that flutters near my heart
XXIII 1

flying
Ripple all thy flying hair.
XXV 6

foam
The foam flies up to be garlanded,
IX 4
And the thunder of horses plunging, foam about their knees:
XXXVI 2

foes
Among his foes in scorn and wrath
XXI 3

fold
Yet must thou fold me unaware
XXVII 3

folded
Together, folded by the night, they lay on earth. I hear
A Prayer 14

folklore
I printed folklore from North and South
Gas 41

follow
Come follow, come follow,
X 3

fond
As thou, fond heart, love's time, so faint, so far,
Tutto 3

footfall
By ways that know the light footfall?
VIII 6

forbearing
Forbearing for old friendship' sake,
XXXIII 4

foreheads
Smoke pluming their foreheads.
Tilly 8

foreign
Of an Irish writer in foreign parts.
Gas 4

foreigner
And the foreigner learns the gift of the gab
Gas 83

foreman
My Irish foreman from Bannockburn
Gas 95

forgive
Forgive your son!
Ecce Puer 16

forgot
He forgot to mention Curly's Hole.
Gas 62

forsaken
O, father forsaken,
Ecce Puer 15

forsook
I, who dishevelled ways forsook
The Holy Office 3

forth
Seemed it of rivers rushing forth
XXVI 5
Forth alone,
XXXV 4
Pluck forth your heart, saltblood, a fruit of tears.
A Memory 13

forwards
Backwards and forwards, down and up,
Gas 7

foul
And I saw the writer's foul intent.
Gas 12

found
Found any soul to fellow his,
XXI 2

fragrant
The fragrant hair,
Tutto 6

frail
Frail the white rose and frail are
A Flower 1

frailest
Rosefrail and fair - yet frailest
A Flower 5

framed
Framed to defy the poison - dart,
XXVII 2

friend
Who was my friend.
XVII 8

friendless
Unfellowed, friendless and alone,
The Holy Office 85

friends
When friends him fail.
XVIII 4
Friends be untrue
XVIII 6

friendship'
Forbearing for old friendship' sake,
XXXIII 4

fringes
With gold - embroidered Celtic fringes --
The Holy Office 28

frivolities
His giddy dames' frivolities
The Holy Office 26

fro
To and fro.
XXXV 12

fruit
Pluck forth your heart, saltflood, a fruit of tears.
A Memory 13

fruits
Your clustered fruits to love's full flood,
Flood 10

full
For lo! the trees are full of sighs
XV 3
Tonight stretch full by the fire!
Tilly 10
Your clustered fruits to love's full flood,
Flood 10

fun
And in a spirit of Irish fun
Gas 17

furrow
From furrow to furrow, while overhead
IX 3

gab
And the foreigner learns the gift of the gab
Gas 83

garden
And come into her little garden
XIII 11
The shadowy garden where love is.
XXIX 8
In the still garden where a child
Simples 3

garlanded
The foam flies up to be garlanded,
IX 4

gate
One who is singing by your gate.
IV 4

gates
The pale gates of sunrise?
III 5

gathering
The year, the year is gathering
XXXIII 18
And, gathering, she sings an air:
Simples 7

gathers
Gathers the simple salad leaves.
Simples 4
Who gathers simples of the moon.
Simples 12

gaunt
Gaunt in gloom,
Nightpiece!

gave
I gave him pain,
XVII 2
Was the kiss she gave to me.
XXXI 8
Her hands that gave
A Flower 2

I gave him for his Irish Review.
Gas 73

gay
Sedate and slow and gay;
II 6
Where the gay winds do most desire
VII 3
There, where the gay winds stay to woo
VII 5
Nor grieve because our love was gay
XXXIII 5

gent
Written by Moore, a genuine gent
Gas 35

gentle
Gentle lady, do not sing
XXVIII 1
In gentle eyes thou veilest,
A Flower 7

gentling
Gentling her awe as to a soul predestined.
A Prayer 5

gently
While sweetly, gently, secretly,
XV 9
Dear eyes that gently me upbraid,
XXIX 2

gents
Ladies and gents, you are here assembled
Gas 1

genuine
Written by Moore, a genuine gent
Gas 35

ghostfires
Ghostfires from heaven's far verges faint illume,
Nightpiece 4

ghosting
At ghosting hour conjurable --
XXVI 10

giddy
His giddy dames' frivolities
The Holy Office 26

gift
And the foreigner learns the gift of the gab
Gas 83

girlish
Bid adieu to girlish days,
XI 2
Thee and woo thy girlish ways --
XI 4
Thy girlish bosom unto him
XI 10

give
My kiss will give peace now
XXXIV 9
Come, give, yield all your strength to me!
A Prayer 2
Myself unto myself will give
The Holy Office 1
'Twould give you a heartburn on your arse:
Gas 40

gladly
Gladly were I a prisoner!
XXII 6

glancing
Loveward above the glancing oar
Watching 2

glass
On the glass;
Ecce Puer 10

gleam
Gleam with a soft and golden fire --
VIII 10

glee
Dancing a ring-around in glee
IX 2

gloom
Through the gloom.
V 12

They cleave the gloom of dreams, a blinding flame,
XXXVI 7

Gaunt in gloom,
Nightpiece 1

In moonless gloom each lapses muted, dim,
Nightpiece 10

glory

Glory and stars beneath his feet --
XII 4

A glory kindles in those eyes,
XII 9

He who hath glory lost, nor hath
XXI 1

glove

Where Christ and Caesar are hand and glove!
Gas 26

glow

The lamp fills with a pale green glow
II 3

gnash

They mouth love's language. Gnash
A Memory 1

go

At that hour when soft lights come and go,
III 13

Go seek her out all courteously,
XIII 1

I pray you go,
XIII 10

And there, love, will we go
XVI 2

Where Love did sometime go.
XVI 4

Lightly come or lightly go:
XXV 1

The ways that we shall go upon.
XXX 8

Where I go.
XXXV 8

The signs that mock me as I go.
Bahnhofstrasse 8

goes

When the shy star goes forth in heaven
IV 1

My love goes slowly, bending to
VII 7

My love goes lightly, holding up
VII 11

Who goes amid the green wood
VIII 1

Who goes amid the merry green wood
VIII 3

going

Staying and going hence,
XXIV 14

Sad as the sea-bird is, when going
XXXV 3

goldbrown

Goldbrown upon the sated flood
Flood 1

gold-embroidered

With gold-embroidered Celtic fringes --
The Holy Office 28

golden

Gleam with a soft and golden fire --
VIII 10

Of grey and golden gossamer.
XV 8

Uplift and sway, O golden vine,
Flood 9

By Gregory of the Golden Mouth:
Gas 42

goldenhair

Goldenhair,
V 2

Goldenhair.
V 16

gone

Love came to us in time gone by
XXX 1

An old man gone.
Ecce Puer 14

good
Now, wind, of your good courtesy
XIII 9

gossamer
Of grey and golden gossamer.
XV 8

graciously
Silently and graciously,
XXIV 3

gradual
Eastward the gradual dawn prevails
XV 5

grammar - book
To hold the poets' grammar - book,
The Holy Office 4

grandmother
Those things for which Grandmother Church
The Holy Office 53

grass
Her shadow on the grass;
VII 8
And on the dappled grass,
XXIV 6

grasses
And heard the prairie grasses sighing:
Watching 3
O hearts, O sighing grasses,
Watching 5

grave
Shy thoughts and grave wide eyes and hands
II 9
In the grave all love shall sleep:
XXVIII 7
We were grave lovers. Love is past
XXX 5
Though they may labour to the grave
The Holy Office 91

greasy
Leave greasy lips their kissing. None
A Memory 10

great
Where the great pine - forest
XX 7
I printed the great John Milicent Synge
Gas 45

greed
Your itch and quailing, nude greed of the flesh.
A Memory 4

green
The lamp fills with a pale green glow
II 3
Who goes amid the green wood
VIII 1
Who goes amid the merry green wood
VIII 3
They come shaking in triumph their long, green hair:
XXXVI 9

Gregory
By Gregory of the Golden Mouth:
Gas 42

grey
Of grey and golden gossamer.
XV 8
From the grey deserts of the north?
XXVI 6
The grey winds, the cold winds are blowing
XXXV 7
At grey moonrise.
She Weeps 4
Grey sea I wrap him warm
On the Beach 6
This grey that stares
A Memory 8
Grey way whose violet signals are
Bahnhofstrasse 3

greygolden
The moon's greygolden meshes make
Alone 1

grief
With joy and grief
Ecce Puer 3

grieve
Nor grieve because our love was gay
XXXIII 5
Grieve not, sweetheart, for anything --
XXXIII 17

grin
Your lean jaws grin with. Lash
Memory 3

groan
The crazy pierstakes groan;
On the Beach 2

groans
I'll penance do with farts and groans
Gas 89

gross
So gross a libel on Stepmother Erin.
Gas 64

grows
O lovely land where the shamrock grows!
Gas 27

guide
My quite illegible railway guide.
Gas 78

had
Ere that mine eyes had learned to weep.
XXIII 10
That had his sweet hours many a one;
XXX 6

hair
Dark leaves on his hair.
I 8
The snood upon thy yellow hair.
XI 6
Of thy hair.
XX 12

hair (continued)
Combing her long hair,
XXIV 2
And still she's combing her long hair
XXIV 7
Comb out your long hair,
XXIV 10
Ripple all thy flying hair.
XXV 6
They come shaking in triumph their long, green hair:
XXXVI 9
The fragrant hair,
Tutto 6
A moondew stars her hanging hair
Simples 5

hand
Her dress with dainty hand.
VII 12
Because within my hand I held
XVII 3
Your hand again.
XVII 4
His hand is under
XVIII 13
We two shall wander, hand in hand,
XXXIII 3
And feels my hand between her thighs
The Holy Office 70
I hold her honour in my hand,
Gas 14
Where Christ and Caesar are hand and glove!
Gas 26
Shall dip his right hand in the urn
Gas 96

hands
Shy thoughts and grave wide eyes and hands
II 9
Her hands that gave
A Flower 2

hanging
A moondew stars her hanging hair
Simples 5

happily
Went murmuring -- O, happily! --
XXXI 6

happiness
And all my happiness.
XXIII 6

happy
Happy Love is come to woo
XI 3
And happy between kiss and kiss;
XXIII 4

hard
And tried so hard to win for us
The Holy Office 45

harps
Of harps playing unto Love to unclose
III 4
Awake to hear the sweet harps play
III 7
Play on, invisible harps, unto Love,
III 11

harsh
Harsh of tongue.
A Memory 7

has
What counsel has the hooded moon
XII 1
So he who has sorrow
XVIII 15
Rain has fallen all the day.
XXXII 1
As his sad heart has lain
She Weeps 10
Raised when she has and shaken
Nightpiece 11
Those souls that hate the strength that mine has
The Holy Office 81

hast
When thou hast heard his name upon
XI 7

hat
Or him who will his hat unfix
The Holy Office 37

hate
Those souls that hate the strength that mine has
The Holy Office 81

hath
He who hath glory lost, nor hath
XXI 1
What sound hath made thy heart to fear?
XXVI 4

have
At that hour when all things have repose,
III 1
I have left my book,
V 9
I have left my room,
V 10
A man shall have sorrow
XVIII 3
Shall have rest.
XVIII 16
For I have heard of witchery
XXIV 11
Nor have I known a love whose praise
XXVII 9
My heart, have you no wisdom thus to despair?
XXXVI 11
My love, my love, my love, why have you left me alone?
XXXVI 12
Blind me with your dark nearness, O have mercy, beloved enemy of my will!
A Prayer 7
Where they have crouched and crawled and prayed
The Holy Office 83
My spirit shall they never have
The Holy Office 92
No, ladies, my press shall have no share in
Gas 63

hazards
Hazards extremes of heterodoxy,
The Holy Office 18

Hazelpatch
To millionaires in Hazelpatch
The Holy Office 34

he
And he is come to visit you.
IV 6
When he at eventide is calling,
IV 8

He sings in the hollow:
X 2
He sings the bolder;
X 10
He is a stranger to me now
XVII 7
For he shall know then
XVIII 5
So he who has sorrow
XVIII 15
He who hath glory lost, nor hath
XXI 1
And all for some strange name he read
XXVI 11
He hears the winds cry to the waters'
XXXV 5
He travels after a winter sun,
Tilly 1
He drives his beasts above Cabra.
Tilly 4
He drives them with a flowering branch before him,
Tilly 7
While they console him when he whinges
The Holy Office 27
He sent me a book ten years ago:
Gas 5
And a play he wrote (you've read it, I'm sure)
Gas 31
In the playboy shift that he pinched as swag
Gas 47
He forgot to mention Curly's Hole.
Gas 62

head
With head to the music bent,
I 10
Her hand inclines this way.
II 8
Like a veil on my head.
XIV 14
My slow life! Bend deeper on me, threatening head,
A Prayer 10
Saw Jesus Christ without his head
The Holy Office 44

hear
Do you hear the night wind and the sighs
III 3

hear (continued)

Awake to hear the sweet harps play
III 7

Hear you amid the drowsy even
IV 3

And hear you not the thrushes calling,
XVI 5

O Sweetheart, hear you
XVIII 1

Now, O now, we hear no more
XXXIII 13

All day I hear the noise of waters
XXXV 1

I hear the noise of many waters
XXXV 9

All day, all night, I hear them flowing
XXXV 11

I hear an army charging upon the land,
XXXVI 1

I moan in sleep when I hear after their whirling laughter.
XXXVI 6

Love, hear thou
She Weeps 5

Together, folded by the night, they lay on earth. I hear
A Prayer 14

To hear why earth and heaven trembled
Gas 2

heard

I heard you singing
V 3

For I heard you singing
V 11

When thou hast heard his name upon
XI 7

Begin (innumerous!) to be heard.
XV 12

For I have heard of witchery
XXIV 11

Is heard in my heart.
XXXIV 4

Is heard at the door.
XXXIV 6

I heard their young hearts crying
Watching 1

And heard the prairie grasses sighing:
Watching 3

hears

He hears the winds cry to the waters'
XXXV 5

heart

Whose song about my heart is falling?
IV 10

I would be ever in that heart
VI 6

So I were ever in that heart.
VI 10

Put in thy heart, my shyly sweet,
XII 2

This heart that flutters near my heart
XXIII 1

Though thy heart presage thee woe,
XXV 2

When the heart is heaviest.
XXV 12

What sound hath made thy heart to fear?
XXVI 4

To know the rapture of thy heart,
XXVII 4

Dear heart, why will you use me so?
XXIX 1

Speak to your heart.
XXXII 8

O you unquiet heart!
XXXIV 2

Is heard in my heart.
XXXIV 4

And quiet to your heart --
XXXIV 10

O you unquiet heart!
XXXIV 12

Clanging, clanging upon the heart as upon an anvil.
XXXVI 8

My heart, have you no wisdom thus to despair?
XXXVI 11

As his sad heart has lain
She Weeps 10

As thou, fond heart, love's time, so faint, so far,
Tutto 3

And in my heart how deep unending
On the Beach 11

And mine a shielded heart for her
Simples 11

Pluck forth your heart, saltblood, a fruit of tears.
A Memory 13

heart (continued)
My heart is torn.
Ecce Puer 4
My heart is as soft as buttermilk.
Gas 70

heartburn
'Twould give you a heartburn on your arse:
Gas 40

hearts
I heard their young hearts crying
Watching 1
O hearts, O sighing grasses,
Watching 5
Dark too our hearts, O love, shall lie and cold
She Weeps 9

heart's
Nor old heart's wisdom yet to know
Bahnhofstrasse 7

heaven
Whose way in heaven is aglow
III 12
When the shy star goes forth in heaven
IV 1
A birdless heaven, seadusk, one lone star
Tutto 1
To enter heaven, travel hell,
The Holy Office 11
To hear why earth and heaven trembled
Gas 2

heaven's
Ghostfires from heaven's far verges faint illume,
Nightpiece 4

heaviest
When the heart is heaviest.
XXV 12

held
Because within my hand I held
XVII 3

hell
To enter heaven, travel hell,
The Holy Office 11

help

I'll burn that book, so help me devil.
Gas 86

hence

Staying and going hence,
XXIV 14

her

Her head inclines this way.
II 8

(O soft I knock and soft entreat her!)
VI 7

Her shadow on the grass;
VII 8

Her dress with dainty hand.
VII 12

With springtide all adorning her?
VIII 2

Go seek her out all courteously,
XIII 1

And come into her little garden
XIII 11

And sing at her window;
XIII 12

Her smooth round breast;
XVIII 14

Combing her long hair,
XXIV 2

And still she's combing her long hair
XXIV 7

Her hands that gave
A Flower 2

A moondew stars her hanging hair
Simples 5

And moonlight kisses her young brow
Simples 6

To shield me from her childish croon
Simples 10

And mine a shielded heart for her
Simples 11

Her thurible.
Nightpiece 12

A name -- her name --
Alone 6

Will choose her what you see to mouth upon.
A Memory 11

her (continued)

Gentling her awe as to a soul predestined.
A Prayer 5

From far her low word breathe on my breaking brain.
A Prayer 15

That shadowy beauty in her eyes,
The Holy Office 64

And feels my hand between her thighs
The Holy Office 70

I hold her honour in my hand,
Gas 14

Her writers and artists to banishment
Gas 16

Betrayed her own leaders, one by one.
Gas 18

Poor sister Scotland! Her doom is fell;
Gas 67

With her tight-breeched British artilleryman
Gas 82

herd

Boor, bond of the herd,
Tilly 9

here

Come! I yield. Bend deeper upon me! I am here.
A Prayer 16

Must here be my interpreter:
The Holy Office 8

Ladies and gents, you are here assembled
Gas 1

That was over here dressed in Austrian yellow,
Gas 50

herring-bone

Indifferent as the herring-bone,
The Holy Office 86

herrings

I love my country -- by herrings I do!
Gas 74

heterodoxy

Hazards extremes of heterodoxy,
The Holy Office 18

hies

With him who hies him to appease
The Holy Office 25

high
That high unconsortable one --
XXI 5
His high Castilian courtesy --
The Holy Office 40
And that high spirit ever wars
The Holy Office 75

highhearted
Highhearted youth comes not again
Bahnhofstrasse 6

him
To Love before him on his way,
III 8
Thy girlish bosom unto him
XI 10
I gave him pain,
XVII 2
When friends him fail.
XVIII 4
But one unto him
XVIII 9
And softly woo him
XVIII 11
He drives them with a flowering branch before him,
Tilly 7
Grey sea I wrap him warm
On the Beach 6
Him who is, him who was!
A Prayer 12
Like him who finds a joy at table
The Holy Office 19
With him who hies him to appease
The Holy Office 25
While they console him when he whinges
The Holy Office 27
Or him who sober all the day
The Holy Office 29
Or him whose conduct "seems to own"
The Holy Office 31
Or him who plays the ragged patch
The Holy Office 33
Or him who will his hat unfix
The Holy Office 37
Or him who loves his Master dear --
The Holy Office 41
Or him who drinks his pint in fear --
The Holy Office 42

him (continued)

Or him who once when snug abed
The Holy Office 43

I gave him for his Irish Review.
Gas 73

his

Pale flowers on his mantle,
I 7

Dark leaves on his hair.
I 8

To Love before him on his way,
III 8

His song is softer than the dew
IV 5

In troop at his shoulder
X 11

When thou hast heard his name upon
XI 7

Glory and stars beneath his feet --
XII 4

For Love is at his noon;
XIII 14

His hand is under
XVIII 13

Found any soul to fellow his,
XXI 2

Among his foes in scorn and wrath
XXI 3

His love is his companion.
XXI 6

Is his, if thou but scan it well,
XXVI 8

That had his sweet hours many a one;
XXX 6

He drives his beasts above Cabra.
Tilly 4

Sad is his voice that calls me, sadly calling,
She Weeps 3

How soft, how sad his voice is ever calling,
She Weeps 6

As his sad heart has lain
She Weeps 10

And touch his trembling fineboned shoulder
On the Beach 7

Dire hunger holds his hour.
A Memory 12

Calm in his cradle
Ecce Puer 5
Unclose his eyes!
Ecce Puer 8
His giddy dames' frivolities
The Holy Office 26
Mixes a naggin in his play --
The Holy Office 30
His preference for a man of "tone" --
The Holy Office 32
Confesses all his pagan past --
The Holy Office 36
Or him who will his hat unfix
The Holy Office 37
His high Castilian courtesy --
The Holy Office 40
Or him who loves his Master dear --
The Holy Office 41
Or him who drinks his pint in fear --
The Holy Office 42
Saw Jesus Christ without his head
The Holy Office 44
From his taxation of contempt.
The Holy Office 78
That lives on his property's ten per cent:
Gas 36
I gave him for his Irish Review.
Gas 73
Shall dip his right hand in the urn
Gas 96

hold
Ah, could they ever hold me there
XXII 5
To hold the poets' grammar-book,
The Holy Office 4
I hold her honour in my hand,
Gas 14

holding
My love goes lightly, holding up
VII 11
Holding to ancient nobleness,
XXI 4

holds
Dire hunger holds his hour.
A Memory 12

Hole

He forgot to mention Curly's Hole.

Gas 62

Holinshead

In Purchas or in Holinshead.

XXVI 12

hollow

He sings in the hollow:

X 2

holy

But weeping after holy fast

The Holy Office 35

And a play on the Word and Holy Paul

Gas 33

home

The voice tells them home is warm.

Tilly 5

homo

Memento homo upon my bum.

Gas 98

honour

I hold her honour in my hand,

Gas 14

hooded

What counsel has the hooded moon

XII 1

hoofs

They moo and make brute music with their hoofs.

Tilly 6

hope

My hope and all my riches is,

XXIII 2

My hope and all my riches -- yes! --

XXIII 5

horses

And the thunder of horses plunging, foam about their knees:

XXXVI 2

hosts
The lost hosts awaken
Nightpiece 8

hour
At that hour when all things have repose,
III 1
At that hour when soft lights come and go,
III 13
At the hour of evenstar
XXV 9
At ghosting hour conjurable --
XXVI 10
Dire hunger holds his hour.
A Memory 12
Spouting Italian by the hour
Gas 51

hours
That had his sweet hours many a one;
XXX 6

how
How sweet to lie there,
XX 5
How love that passes is enough.
XXVIII 4
Of lovers that are dead, and how
XXVIII 6
How is your beauty raimented!
XXIX 4
How soft, how sad his voice is ever calling,
She Weeps 6
And in my heart how deep unending
On the Beach 11
How can one fail to be intense?
The Holy Office 22

hum
The wild bees hum.
X 12

humour
'Twas Irish humour, wet and dry,
Gas 19

hundred
I read it a hundred times or so,
Gas 6

hundred (continued)
Of one hundred pounds on the estimate
Gas 72

hunger
Dire hunger holds his hour.
A Memory 12

hurry
O, hurry over the dark lands
XIII 5

I
'Tis I that am your visitant.
IV 12
I heard you singing
V 3
I read no more,
V 6
I have left my book,
V 9
I have left my room,
V 10
For I heard you singing
V 11
I would in that sweet bosom be
VI 1
VI 5
I would be ever in that heart
VI 6
(O soft I knock and soft entreat her!)
VI 7
So I were ever in that heart.
VI 10
Sweetheart, I come.
X 16
And say I come,
XIII 2
I pray you go,
XIII 10
I wait by the cedar tree,
XIV 9
I gave him pain,
XVII 2
Because within my hand I held
XVII 3
I would we lay,
XX 2

Gladly were I a prisoner!
XXII 6
I laid those treasures I possessed
XXIII 9
I pray you, cease to comb out,
XXIV 9
For I have heard of witchery
XXIV 11
Though I thy Mithridates were,
XXVII 1
And I but render and confess
XXVII 5
Nor have I known a love whose praise
XXVII 9
My love and I did walk together;
XXXI 3
Come, my beloved, where I may
XXXII 7
All day I hear the noise of waters
XXXV 1
Where I go.
XXXV 8
I hear the noise of many waters
XXXV 9
All day, all night, I hear them flowing
XXXV 11
I hear an army charging upon the land,
XXXVI 1
I moan in sleep when I hear afar their whirling laughter.
XXXVI 6
I bleed by the black stream
Tilly 11
I heard their young hearts crying
Watching 1
Grey sea I wrap him warm
On the Beach 6
Be mine, I pray, a waxen ear
Simples 9
Whereto I pass at eve of day,
Bahnhofstrasse 2
The signs that mock me as I go.
Bahnhofstrasse 8
I dare not withstand the cold touch that I dread.
A Prayer 8
Together, folded by the night, they lay on earth. I hear
A Prayer 14
Come! I yield. Bend deeper upon me! I am here.
A Prayer 16

I (continued)
I, who dishevelled ways forsook
The Holy Office 3
But I must not accounted be
The Holy Office 23
But all these men of whom I speak
The Holy Office 47
I carry off their filthy streams
The Holy Office 50
For I can do those things for them
The Holy Office 51
Through which I lost my diadem,
The Holy Office 52
Thus I relieve their timid arses,
The Holy Office 55
I act as vicar-general
The Holy Office 60
I do a similar kind service.
The Holy Office 62
For I detect without surprise
The Holy Office 63
So distantly I turn to view
The Holy Office 79
I stand, the self-doomed, unafraid,
The Holy Office 84
I flash my antlers on the air.
The Holy Office 88
I read it a hundred times or so,
Gas 6
I printed it all to the very last word
Gas 9
And I saw the writer's foul intent.
Gas 12
But I owe a duty to Ireland:
Gas 13
I hold her honour in my hand,
Gas 14
To show you for strictures I don't care a button
Gas 29
I printed the poems of Mountainy Mutton
Gas 30
And some woman's legs that I can't recall,
Gas 34
I printed mystical books in dozens:
Gas 37
I printed the table-book of Cousins
Gas 38

I printed folklore from North and South
Gas 41
I printed poets, sad, silly and solemn:
Gas 43
I printed Patrick What-do-you-Colm:
Gas 44
I printed the great John Milicent Synge
Gas 45
But I draw the line at that bloody fellow
Gas 49
I'm damned if I do -- I'm damned to blazes!
Gas 59
I pity the poor -- that's why I took
Gas 65
Colm can tell you I made a rebate
Gas 71
I gave him for his Irish Review.
Gas 73
I love my country -- by herrings I do!
Gas 74
I wish you could see what tears I weep
Gas 75
When I think of the emigrant train and ship.
Gas 76
That's why I publish far and wide
Gas 77
I'll sing a psalm as I watch it burn
Gas 87
This very next lent I will unbare
Gas 91
My awful sin I will confess.
Gas 94

if
Is his, if thou but scan it well,
XXVI 8
I'm damned if I do -- I'm damned to blazes!
Gas 59

I'll
Shite and onions! Do you think I'll print
Gas 55
I'll burn that book, so help me devil.
Gas 86
I'll sing a psalm as I watch it burn
Gas 87
And the ashes I'll keep in a one-handled urn.
Gas 88

I'll (continued)
I'll penance do with farts and groans
Gas 89

illegible
My quite illegible railway guide.
Gas 78

illume
Ghostfires from heaven's far verges faint illume,
Nightpiece 4

I'm
And a play he wrote (you've read it, I'm sure)
Gas 31
I'm damned if I do -- I'm damned to blazes!
Gas 59

imprisonment
Of that so sweet imprisonment
XXII 1

incense
As the bleak incense surges, cloud on cloud,
Nightpiece 16

incertitude
Incertitude!
Flood 12

inclines
Her head inclines this way.
II 8

indifferent
Indifferent as the herring-bone,
The Holy Office 86

indulgences
Of plenary indulgences.
The Holy Office 14

ingle-nook
Who safe at ingle-nook, by proxy,
The Holy Office 17

innumerous
Begin (innumerous!) to be heard.
XV 12

institute
In the porch of my printing institute
Gas 79

instrument
Upon an instrument.
I 12

intense
How can one fail to be intense?
The Holy Office 22

intent
And I saw the writer's foul intent.
Gas 12

interpreter
Must here be my interpreter:
The Holy Office 8

interwoven
Dearest, through interwoven arms
XXII 7

into
And come into her little garden
XIII 11
Flung quicklime into Parnell's eye;
Gas 20

invisible
Play on, invisible harps, unto Love,
III 11

Ireland
But I owe a duty to Ireland:
Gas 13
O Ireland my first and only love
Gas 25

Irish
Of an Irish writer in foreign parts.
Gas 4
And in a spirit of Irish fun
Gas 17
'Twas Irish humour, wet and dry,
Gas 19
'Tis Irish brains that save from doom
Gas 21

Irish (continued)
Talk about Irish Names of Places!
Gas 60
I gave him for his Irish Review.
Gas 73
My Irish foreman from Bannockburn
Gas 95

irreverent
Till the irreverent mountain air
XXV 5

is
Till night is overgone?
III 10
Whose way in heaven is aglow
III 12
One who is singing by your gate.
IV 4
His song is softer than the dew
IV 5
And he is come to visit you.
IV 6
When he at eventide is calling,
IV 8
Whose song about my heart is falling?
IV 10
(O sweet it is and fair it is!)
VI 2
My love is in a light attire
VII 1
O, it is for my true love
VIII 13
O, it is for my own true love,
VIII 15
That is so young and fair.
VIII 16
Love is unhappy when love is away!
IX 9
Dreams is over --
X 14
Happy Love is come to woo
XI 3
That is the sign of maidenhood.
XI 12
A sage that is but kith and kin
XII 5
Wind of spices whose song is ever
XIII 3

Singing: The bridal wind is blowing
XIII 13
For Love is at his noon;
XIII 14
O cool is the valley now
XVI 1
For many a choir is singing now
XVI 3
O cool and pleasant is the valley
XVI 7
There is no word nor any sign
XVII 5
He is a stranger to me now
XVII 7
His hand is under
XVIII 13
Enaisled is!
XX 8
His love is his companion.
XXI 6
My soul, dearest, is fain --
XXII 2
My hope and all my riches is,
XXIII 2
The sun is in the willow leaves
XXIV 5
When the heart is heaviest.
XXV 12
Is his, if thou but scan it well,
XXVI 8
How love that passes is enough.
XXVIII 4
Love is aweary now.
XXVIII 8
How is your beauty raimented!
XXIX 4
The shadowy garden where love is.
XXIX 8
For Love at first is all afraid.
XXX 4
We were grave lovers. Love is past
XXX 5
Which now is ended in this way.
XXXIII 6
Is knocking, knocking at the tree;
XXXIII 8
The wind is whistling merrily.
XXXIII 10

is (continued)

The year, the year is gathering
XXXIII 18

Is heard in my heart.
XXXIV 4

Is heard at the door.
XXXIV 6

Is crying "Sleep no more."
XXXIV 8

Sad as the sea-bird is, when going
XXXV 3

The voice tells them home is warm.
Tilly 5

Whose soul is sere and paler
A Flower 3

Sad is his voice that calls me, sadly calling,
She Weeps 3

How soft, how sad his voice is ever calling,
She Weeps 6

Fair as the wave is, fair, art thou!
Simples 8

Lambent and vast and ruthless as is thine
Flood 11

And all my soul is a delight,
Alone 7

Love's breath in you is stale, worded or sung,
A Memory 5

Him who is, him who was!
A Prayer 12

A child is born
Ecce Puer 2

My heart is torn.
Ecce Puer 4

Young life is breathed
Ecce Puer 9

A child is sleeping:
Ecce Puer 13

A Dante is, unprejudiced,
The Holy Office 16

Knows the soft flame that is desire.
The Holy Office 72

Let them continue as is meet
The Holy Office 89

Poor sister Scotland! Her doom is fell;
Gas 66

My conscience is fine as Chinese silk:
Gas 69

My heart is as soft as buttermilk.
Gas 70

it
(O sweet it is and fair it is!)
VI 2
To make it merrier?
VIII 4
O, it is for my true love
VIII 13
O, it is for my own true love,
VIII 15
Seemed it of rivers rushing forth
XXVI 5
Is his, if thou but scan it well,
XXVI 8
O, it was out by Donnycarney
XXXI 1
She never seems to think of it;
The Holy Office 68
I read it a hundred times or so,
Gas 6
I printed it all to the very last word
Gas 9
And a play he wrote (you've read it, I'm sure)
Gas 31
Who was it said: Resist not evil?
Gas 85
I'll sing a psalm as I watch it burn
Gas 87

Italian
Spouting Italian by the hour
Gas 51

itch
Your itch and quailing, nude greed of the flesh.
A Memory 4

its
Sways and uplifts its weedy mane
Flood 6
Its cruel calm, submission's misery,
A Prayer 4

It's
It's a wonder to me, upon my soul,
Gas 61

jam
Downes's cakeshop and Williams's jam?
Gas 58

jaws
Your lean jaws grin with. Lash
A Memory 3

Jesus
Saw Jesus Christ without his head
The Holy Office 44

John
I printed the great John Milicent Synge
Gas 45
To O'Leary Curtis and John Wyse Power
Gas 52

joy
Subduer, do not leave me! Only joy, only anguish,
A Prayer 17
With joy and grief
Ecce Puer 3
Like him who finds a joy at table
The Holy Office 19

katharsis
Perform my office of Katharsis.
The Holy Office 56

Katharsis-Purgative
This name, Katharsis-Purgative.
The Holy Office 2

keep
The wrens will divers treasures keep,
XXIII 8
A red-headed Scotchman to keep my book.
Gas 66
And the ashes I'll keep in a one-handled urn.
Gas 88

keys
She bends upon the yellow keys,
II 7

kin
A sage that is but kith and kin
XII 5

kind
I do a similar kind service.
The Holy Office 62

kindles
A glory kindles in those eyes,
XII 9

kiss
Sweet to kiss,
XX 6
Thy kiss descending
XX 9
And happy between kiss and kiss;
XXIII 4
Through the soft cry of kiss to kiss,
XXIX 6
Was the kiss she gave to me.
XXXI 8
Yet will we kiss, sweetheart, before
XXXIII 15
My kiss will give peace now
XXXIV 9

kisses
And moonlight kisses her young brow
Simples 6

kissing
Leave greasy lips their kissing. None
A Memory 10

kith
A sage that is but kith and kin
XII 5

kneeling
Kneeling upon my marrowbones.
Gas 90

knees
And the thunder of horses plunging, foam about their knees:
XXXVI 2

knock
(O soft I knock and soft entreat her!)
VI 7

knocking
Is knocking, knocking at the tree;
XXXIII 8

know
Know you by this, the lover's chant,
IV 11
By ways that know the light footfall?
VIII 6
For he shall know then
XVIII 5
To know the rapture of thy heart,
XXVII 4
Calling to them, a voice they know,
Tilly 3
Nor old heart's wisdom yet to know
Bahnhofstrasse 7

known
Nor have I known a love whose praise
XXVII 9

knows
Knows the soft flame that is desire.
The Holy Office 72
For everyone knows the Pope can't belch
Gas 23

labour
Though they may labour to the grave
The Holy Office 91

laburnum
Laburnum tendrils trail.
Alone 4

laden
O come among the laden trees:
XXXII 2

ladies
Ladies and gents, you are here assembled
Gas 1
(Allow me, ladies, to blow my nose)
Gas 28
No, ladies, my press shall have no share in
Gas 63

lady
Dear lady, a divining ear.
XXVI 2
Gentle lady, do not sing
XXVIII 1

laid
I laid those treasures I possessed
XXIII 9

lain
As his sad heart has lain
She Weeps 10

lake
The shorelamps in the sleeping lake
Alone 3

lambent
Vast wings above the lambent waters brood
Flood 3
Lambent and vast and ruthless as is thine
Flood 11

lamp
The lamp fills with a pale green glow
II 3

land
Over the laughing land,
VII 10
For seas and land shall not divide us
XIII 7
Now, O now, in this brown land
XXXIII 1
I hear an army charging upon the land,
XXXVI 1
This lovely land that always sent
Gas 15
O lovely land where the shamrock grows!
Gas 27

lands
O, hurry over the dark lands
XIII 5

language
They mouth love's language. Gnash.
A Memory 1

lapses
In moonless gloom each lapses muted, dim,
Nightpiece 10

lash
Your lean jaws grin with. Lash
A Memory 3

last
Welcome to us now at the last
XXX 7
I printed it all to the very last word
Gas 9

laughing
Over the laughing land,
VII 10

laughter
That song and laughter
X 7
Oread, let thy laughter run,
XXV 4
Love and laughter song-confessed
XXV 11
I moan in sleep when I hear afar their whirling laughter.
XXXVI 6

lay
I would we lay,
XX 2
Lay aside sadness and sing
XXVIII 3
Together, folded by the night, they lay on earth. I hear
A Prayer 14

leaders
Betrayed her own leaders, one by one.
Gas 18

leaky
The leaky barge of the Bishop of Rome
Gas 22

lean
Lean out of the window,
V 1
V 15

Your lean jaws grin with. Lash
A Memory 3

leanest
Thou leanest to the shell of night,
XXVI 1

learned
Ere that mine eyes had learned to weep.
XXIII 10

learns
And the foreigner learns the gift of the gab
Gas 83

leave
Leave dreams to the dreamers
X 5
We take sad leave at close of day.
XXXIII 16
Leave greasy lips their kissing. None
A Memory 10
Subduer, do not leave me! Only joy, only anguish,
A Prayer 17

leaves
Dark leaves on his hair.
I 8
The young leaves as they pass,
VII 6
Whose leaves the morn admonisheth.
XV 4
The sun is in the willow leaves
XXIV 5
The leaves lie thick upon the way
XXXII 3
The leaves -- they do not sigh at all
XXXIII 11
Gathers the simple salad leaves.
Simples 4
My scarlet leaves them white as wool:
The Holy Office 57

left
I have left my book,
V 9
I have left my room,
V 10

left (continued)
My love, my love, my love, why have you left me alone?
XXXVI 12
Left me severely in the lurch.
The Holy Office 54

legs
And some woman's legs that I can't recall,
Gas 34

lent
This very next lent I will unbare
Gas 91

lest
Lest bards in the attempt should err
The Holy Office 7

let
Oread, let thy laughter run,
XXV 4
Let them continue as is meet
The Holy Office 89

Leviathan
The uses of Leviathan
The Holy Office 74

libel
So gross a libel on Stepmother Erin.
Gas 64

lie
How sweet to lie there,
XX 5
The leaves lie thick upon the way
XXXII 3
Dark too our hearts, O love, shall lie and cold
She Weeps 9

lies
The night-dew lies
XIV 3
The pale dew lies
XIV 13
Where soul with soul lies prisoned.
XXII 12

Where my dark lover lies.
She Weeps 2
Lies not, stark skin and bone.
A Memory 9
The living lies.
Ecce Puer 6
At night when close in bed she lies
The Holy Office 69

life
My slow life! Bend deeper on me, threatening head.
A Prayer 10
Young life is breathed
Ecce Puer 9
Ruling one's life by common sense
The Holy Office 21

lift
The rockvine clusters lift and sway.
Flood 2

light
My love is in a light attire
VII 1
By ways that know the light footfall?
VIII 6
My little love in light attire
The Holy Office 71

lightly
My love goes lightly, holding up
VII 11
Lightly come or lightly go:
XXV 1
Lightly, lightly -- ever so:
XXV 7

lights
With lights of amethyst.
II 12
At that hour when soft lights come and go,
III 13

like
Like a veil on my head.
XIV 14
Like him who finds a joy at table
The Holy Office 19

line

But I draw the line at the bloody fellow
Gas 49

lip

Wherefore receive now from my lip
The Holy Office 9

lips

Upon my lips and eyes.
XIV 4

Dearest, my lips wax all too wise;
XXVII 8

Leave greasy lips their kissing. None
A Memory 10

list

That wander as they list --
II 10

little

And come into her little garden
XIII 11

And a little ashes
XVIII 7

Ever so little falsity
XXVII 12

Staying a little by the way
XXXII 5

My little love in light attire
The Holy Office 71

live

Though love live but a day?
XXIII 12

lives

Their lives ascend as a continual sigh.
XIX 6

That lives on his property's ten per cent:
Gas 36

living

The living lies.
Ecce Puer 6

lo

For lo! the trees are full of sighs
XV 3

lone
A birdless heaven, seadusk, one lone star
Tutto 1

loneliness
And all around our loneliness
XXXIII 9

lonely
O lonely watcher of the skies,
III 2

long
Coming her long hair,
XXIV 2
And still she's combing her long hair
XXIV 7
Comb out your long hair,
XXIV 10
Sing about the long deep sleep
XXVIII 5
They come shaking in triumph their long, green hair:
XXXVI 9
And long and loud,
Nightpiece 13

long-lost
The long-lost works of Aeschylus.
The Holy Office 46

look
The clear young eyes' soft look, the candid brow,
Tutto 5

looking-glass
Before the looking-glass.
XXIV 8

Lord
But by the mercy of the Lord
Gas 10

lost
He who hath glory lost, nor hath
XXI 1
The lost hosts awaken
Nightpiece 8

lost (continued)
Through which I lost my diadem,
The Holy Office 52

loud
And long and loud,
Nightpiece 13

love
For Love wanders there,
I 6
Of harps playing unto Love to unclose
III 4
To Love before him on his way,
III 8
Play on, invisible harps, unto Love,
III 11
My love is in a light attire
VII 1
My love goes slowly, bending to
VII 7
My love goes lightly, holding up
VII 11
O, it is for my true love
VIII 13
O, it is for my own true love,
VIII 15
Saw you my true love anywhere?
IX 6
Love is unhappy when love is away!
IX 9
All you that love.
X 4
Happy Love is come to woo
XI 3
Of Love in ancient plenilune,
XII 3
My love and me.
XIII 8
For Love is at his noon;
XIII 14
And soon will your true love be with you,
XIII 15
My sister, my love.
XIV 10
And there, love, will we go
XVI 2

love (continued)

Where Love did sometime go.
XVI 4

And there, love, will we stay.
XVI 8

In ways of love.
XVIII 12

Sweet love, away.
XX 16

His love is his companion.
XXI 6

By love made tremulous,
XXII 8

Though love live but a day?
XXIII 12

Love and laughter song-confessed
XXV 11

Nor have I known a love whose praise
XXVII 9

Neither a love where may not be
XXVII 11

Sad songs about the end of love;
XXVIII 2

How love that passes is enough.
XXVIII 4

In the grave all love shall sleep:
XXVIII 7

Love is aweary now.
XXVIII 8

The shadowy garden where love is.
XXIX 8

And soon shall love dissolved by
XXIX 9

But you, dear love, too dear to me,
XXIX 11

Love came to us in time gone by
XXX 1

For Love at first is all afraid.
XXX 4

We were grave lovers. Love is past
XXX 5

My love and I did walk together;
XXXI 3

Where Love did so sweet music make
XXXIII 2

Nor grieve because our love was gay
XXXIII 5

love (continued)

My love, my love, my love, why have you left me alone?
XXXVI 12

Love, hear thou
She Weeps 5

Dark too our hearts, O love, shall lie and cold
She Weeps 9

When the dear love she yielded with a sigh
Tutto 11

Aches of love!
On the Beach 12

Cease, silent love! My doom!
A Prayer 6

May love and mercy
Ecce Puer 7

My little love in light attire
The Holy Office 71

O Ireland my first and only love
Gas 25

I love my country -- by herrings I do!
Gas 74

loveblown

Vainly your loveblown bannerets mourn!
Watching 6

lovely

This lovely land that always sent
Gas 15

O lovely land where the shamrock grows!
Gas 27

lover

As lover to lover,
X 15

That makes as one thing to the lover
XXIV 13

Where my dark lover lies.
She Weeps 2

lovers

Of lovers that are dead, and how
XXVIII 6

We were grave lovers. Love is past
XXX 5

lover's

Know you by this, the lover's chant,
IV 11

Your lover's tale;
XVIII 2

loves
Or him who loves his Master dear --
The Holy Office 41

love's
From love's deep slumber and from death,
XV 2
As thou, fond heart, love's time, so faint, so far,
Tutto 3
Your clustered fruits to love's full flood,
Flood 10
They mouth love's language. Gnash
A Memory 1
Love's breath in you is stale, worded or sung,
A Memory 5

loveward
Loveward above the glancing oar
Watching 2

low
From far a low word breathes on the breaking brain
A Prayer 3
From far her low word breathe on my breaking brain.
A Prayer 15

lowliest
Lowliest attendants are;
XXV 10

lurch
Left me severely in the lurch.
The Holy Office 54

lures
Sweet lures, repine
Tutto 10

lying
Prefer a lying clamour before you:
XIX 2

mad
Who a mad tale bequeaths to us
XXVI 9

made
By love made tremulous,
XXII 8
What sound hath made thy heart to fear?
XXVI 4
Colm can tell you I made a rebate
Gas 71

Mahamanvantara
Till the Mahamanvantara be done:
The Holy Office 94

maiden
And for each maiden, shy and nervous,
The Holy Office 61

maidenhood
That is the sign of maidenhood.
XI 12
The "dare not" of sweet maidenhood
The Holy Office 65

maidenly
All maidenly, disconsolate,
IV 2

make
Make music sweet;
I 2
To make it merrier?
VIII 4
Can make amend --
XVII 6
Where Love did so sweet music make
XXXIII 2
They moo and make brute music with their hoofs.
Tilly 6
The moon's grey goldenmeshes make
Alone 1
Make me the sewer of their clique.
The Holy Office 48
Nor make my soul with theirs as one
The Holy Office 93

makes
That makes as one thing to the lover
XXIV 13

making
Making to tremble all those veils
XV 7
Making moan,
XXXV 2

malice
The malice of thy tenderness.
XXVII 6

malt
Neither to malt nor crucifix
The Holy Office 38

Mammon
But Mannon places under ban
The Holy Office 73

Mammon's
On Mammon's countless servitors
The Holy Office 76

man
A man shall have sorrow
XVIII 3
An old man gone.
Ecce Puer 14
His preference for a man of "tone" --
The Holy Office 32

manager's
From Maunsel's manager's travelling bag.
Gas 48

mane
Sways and uplifts its weedy mane
Flood 6

manner
In a manner no blackamoor printer could bear.
Gas 54

mantle
Pale flowers on his mantle,
I 7

many
For many a choir is singing now
XVI 3

many (continued)
With many a pretty air.
XXIV 4
All fair, with many a pretty air
XXIV 15
And many a negligence.
XXIV 16
Vales and many a wasted sun,
XXV 3
That had his sweet hours many a one;
XXX 6
I hear the noise of many waters
XXXV 9

marrowbones
Kneeling upon my marrowbones.
Gas 90

Master
Or him who loves his Master dear --
The Holy Office 41

Maunsel's
From Maunsel's manager's travelling bag.
Gas 48

may
Nor muse: Who may this singer be
IV 9
Nowise may trouble us;
XXII 10
Neither a love where may not be
XXVII 11
Come, my beloved, where I may
XXXII 7
May love and mercy
Ecce Puer 7
That they may dream their dreamy dreams
The Holy Office 49
Though they may labour to the grave
The Holy Office 91

May
Winds of May, that dance on the sea,
IX 1
For the winds of May!
IX 8

me

Where no rude wind might visit me.
VI 3
Believe me rather that am wise
XII 7
My love and me.
XIII 8
He is a stranger to me now
XVII 7
Come with me now,
XX 15
Soft arms that woo me to relent
XXII 3
And woo me to detain.
XXII 4
Ah, could they ever hold me there
XXII 5
That night allures me where alarms
XXII 9
Yet must thou fold me unaware
XXVII 3
Dear heart, why will you use me so?
XXIX 1
Dear eyes that gently me upbraid,
XXIX 2
But you, dear love, too dear to me,
XXIX 11
Alas! why will you use me so?
XXIX 12
And sweet were the words she said to me.
XXXI 4
Was the kiss she gave to me.
XXXI 8
My love, my love, my love, why have you left me alone?
XXXVI 12
Sad is his voice that calls me, sadly calling,
She Weeps 3
To shield me from her childish croon
Simples 10
The eyes that mock me sign the way
Bahnhofstrasse 1
The signs that mock me as I go.
Bahnhofstrasse 8
Come, give, yield all your strength to me!
A Prayer 2
Blind me with your dark nearness, O have mercy, beloved enemy of my will!
A Prayer 7

me (continued)

Draw from me still
A Prayer 9

My slow life! Bend deeper on me, threatening head,
A Prayer 10

Come! I yield. Bend deeper upon me! I am here.
A Prayer 16

Subduer, do not leave me! Only joy, only anguish,
A Prayer 17

Take me, save me, soothe me, O spare me!
A Prayer 18

Make me the sewer of their clique.
The Holy Office 48

Left me severely in the lurch.
The Holy Office 54

Through me they purge a bellyful.
The Holy Office 58

And though they spurn me from their door
The Holy Office 95

He sent me a book ten years ago:
Gas 5

(Allow me, ladies, to blow my nose)
Gas 28

It's a wonder to me, upon my soul,
Gas 61

I'll burn that book, so help me devil.
Gas 86

meet

The willows meet.
I 4

Whenever publicly we meet
The Holy Office 67

Let them continue as is meet
The Holy Office 89

memento

Memento homo upon my bum.
Gas 98

memories

Of memories.
XXXII 4

Of memories shall we depart.
XXXII 6

men

Be not sad because all men
XIX 1

But all these men of whom I speak
The Holy Office 47

mention
He forgot to mention Curly's Hole.
Gas 62

mercy
Blind me with your dark nearness, O have mercy, beloved enemy of my will!
A Prayer 7
May love and mercy
Ecce Puer 7
But by the mercy of the Lord
Gas 10

merrier
To make it merrier?
VIII 4

merrily
The wind is whistling merrily.
XXXIII 10

merry
A merry air.
V 4
A merry air,
V 14
Who goes amid the merry green wood
VIII 3

meshes
The moon's greygolden meshes make
Alone 1

mien
With mien so virginal?
VIII 8

might
Where no rude wind might visit me.
VI 3
Where only peace might be my part.
VI 8

mild
Of cool sweet dew and radiance mild
Simples 1

Milicent
I printed the great John Milicent Synge
Gas 45

millionaires
To millionaires in Hazelpatch
The Holy Office 34

mind
The mind of witty Aristotle,
The Holy Office 6
The darkness of my mind was rent
Gas 11

mine
Trembles to starlight. Mine, O Mine!
XII 10
Ere that mine eyes had learned to weep.
XXIII 10
Be mine, I pray, a waxen ear
Simples 9
And mine a shielded heart for her
Simples 11
Those souls that hate the strength that mine has
The Holy Office 81

mirror
Through the clear mirror of your eyes,
XXIX 5

misery
Its cruel calm, submission's misery,
A Prayer 4

mist
No more be tears in moon or mist
XII 11

Mithridates
Though I thy Mithridates were,
XXVII 1

mixes
Mixes a naggin in his play --
The Holy Office 30

moan
Making moan,
XXXV 2
I moan in sleep when I hear afar their whirling laughter.
XXXVI 6

mock
The eyes that mock me sign the way
Bahnhofstrasse 1
The signs that mock me as I go.
Bahnhofstrasse 8

monotone
Monotone.
XXXV 6

monument
The name of the Wellington Monument,
Gas 56

moo
They moo and make brute music with their hoofs.
Tilly 6

mood
That mood of thine, O timorous,
XXVI 7

moon
What counsel has the hooded moon
XII 1
No more be tears in moon or mist
XII 11
The moon a web of silence weaves
Simples 2
Who gathers simples of the moon.
Simples 12

moondew
A moondew stars her hanging hair
Simples 5

moongrey
Under the moongrey nettles, the black mould
She Weeps 11

moonless
In moonless gloom each lapses muted, dim,
Nightpiece 10

moonlight
And moonlight kisses her young brow
Simples 6

moonrise
At grey moonrise.
She Weeps 4

moon's
The moon's greygolden meshes make
Alone 1

Moore
Written by Moore, a genuine gent
Gas 35

more
O bend no more in revery
IV 7

I read no more,
V 6

No more be tears in moon or mist
XII 11

Now, O now, we hear no more
XXXIII 13

Is crying "Sleep no more."
XXXIV 8

No more, return no more!
Watching 4

No more will the wild wind that passes
Watching 7

Return, no more return.
Watching 8

She cannot find any more Stuarts to sell.
Gas 68

morn
Whose leaves the morn admonisheth.
XV 4

The flowery bells of morn are stirred
XV 10

mossy
For there, as in some mossy nest
XXIII 7

most
Where the gay winds do most desire
VII 3

motley
The shamblings of that motley crew,
The Holy Office 80

mould
Under the moongrey nettles, the black mould
She Weeps 11

mountain
Till the irreverent mountain air
XXV 5

mountain-ridges
Firm as the mountain-ridges where
The Holy Office 87

Mountainy
I printed the poems of Mountainy Mutton
Gas 30

mourn
Vainly your loveblown bannerets mourn!
Watching 6

mouth
They mouth love's language. Gnash
A Memory 1
Will choose her what you see to mouth upon.
A Memory 11
By Gregory of the Golden Mouth:
Gas 42

move
Do nothing move.
X 8
Will softly move
XVIII 10

mummers

To sister mummers one and all
The Holy Office 59

mumming

One of that mumming company --
The Holy Office 24

murmuring

Went murmuring -- O, happily! --
XXXI 6

muse

Nor muse: Who may this singer be
IV 9

music

Make music sweet;
I 2

There's music along the river
I 5

With head to the music bent,
I 10

Soft sweet music in the air above
III 14

A music of sighs:
XIV 6

Where Love did so sweet music make
XXXIII 2

They moo and make brute music with their hoofs.
Tilly 6

must

Yet must thou fold me unaware
XXVII 3

Must here be my interpreter:
The Holy Office 8

But I must not accounted be
The Holy Office 23

muted

In moonless gloom each lapses muted, dim,
Nightpiece 10

muttering

And muttering rain.
She Weeps 12

Mutton

I printed the poems of Mountainy Mutton
Gas 30

my

Whose song about my heart is falling?
IV 10

My book was closed;
V 5

I have left my book,
V 9

I have left my room,
V 10

Where only peace might be my part.
VI 8

My love is in a light attire
VII 1

My love goes slowly, bending to
VII 7

My love goes lightly, holding up
VII 11

O, it is for my true love
VIII 13

O, it is for my own true love,
VIII 15

Saw you my true love anywhere?
IX 6

Put in thy heart, my shyly sweet,
XII 2

My love and me.
XIII 8

My dove, my beautiful one,
XIV 1

Upon my lips and eyes.
XIV 4

My dove, my beautiful one!
XIV 8

My sister, my love.
XIV 10

My breast shall be your bed.
XIV 12

Like a veil on my head.
XIV 14

My fair one, my fair dove,
XIV 15

From dewy dreams, my soul, arise
XV 1

my (continued)
Because your voice was at my side
XVII 1
Because within my hand I held
XVII 3
Who was my friend.
XVII 8
My soul, dearest, is fain --
XXII 2
This heart that flutters near my heart
XXIII 1
My hope and all my riches is,
XXIII 2
My hope and all my riches -- yes! --
XXIII 5
And all my happiness.
XXIII 6
Dearest, my lips wax all too wise;
XXVII 8
My love and I did walk together;
XXXI 3
And sweet were the words she said to me.
XXXI 4
Come, my beloved, where I may
XXXII 7
Is heard in my heart.
XXXIV 4
My kiss will give peace now
XXXIV 9
My heart, have you no wisdom thus to despair?
XXXVI 11
My love, my love, my love, why have you left me alone?
XXXVI 12
For my torn bough!
Tilly 12
My blueveined child.
A Flower 8
Where my dark lover lies.
She Weeps 2
And in my heart how deep unending
On the Beach 11
And all my soul is a delight,
Alone 7
Cease, silent love! My doom!
A Prayer 6
Blind me with your dark nearness, O have mercy, beloved enemy of my will!
A Prayer 7

My slow life! Bend deeper on me, threatening head,
A Prayer 10
Proud by my downfall, remembering, pitying
A Prayer 11
From far her low word breathe on my breaking brain.
A Prayer 15
My heart is torn.
Ecce Puer 4
Must here be my interpreter:
The Holy Office 8
Wherefore receive now from my lip
The Holy Office 9
Through which I lost my diadem,
The Holy Office 52
Perform my office of Katharsis.
The Holy Office 56
My scarlet leaves them white as wool:
The Holy Office 57
That answers my corruptive "would."
The Holy Office 66
And feels my hand between her thighs
The Holy Office 70
My little love in light attire
The Holy Office 71
I flash my antlers on the air.
The Holy Office 88
My spirit shall they never have
The Holy Office 92
Nor make my soul with theirs as one
The Holy Office 93
My soul shall spurn them evermore.
The Holy Office 96
The darkness of my mind was rent
Gas 11
I hold her honour in my hand,
Gas 14
O Ireland my first and only love
Gas 25
(Allow me, ladies, to blow my nose)
Gas 28
It's a wonder to me, upon my soul,
Gas 61
No, ladies, my press shall have no share in
Gas 63
A red-headed Scotchman to keep my book.
Gas 66
My conscience is fine as Chinese silk:
Gas 69

my (continued)
My heart is as soft as buttermilk.
Gas 70
I love my country -- by herrings I do!
Gas 74
My quite illegible railway guide.
Gas 78
In the porch of my printing institute
Gas 79
My penitent buttocks to the air
Gas 92
And sobbing beside my printing press
Gas 93
My awful sin I will confess
Gas 94
My Irish foreman from Bannockburn
Gas 95
Memento homo upon my bum.
Gas 98

myself
Myself unto myself will give
The Holy Office 1

mystical
I printed mystical books in dozens:
Gas 37

mysticist
For every true-born mysticist
The Holy Office 15

naggin
Mixes a naggin in his play --
The Holy Office 30

name
When thou hast heard his name upon
XI 7
And all for some strange name he read
XXVI 11
A name -- her name --
Alone 6
This name, Katharsis - Purgative.
The Holy Office 2
The name of the Wellington Monument,
Gas 56

names
  Talk about Irish Names of Places!
    Gas 60

nave
  Night's sindark nave.
    Nightpiece 6
  To night's nave upsoaring,
    Nightpiece 14

near
  This heart that flutters near my heart
    XXIII 1

nearness
  Blind me with your dark nearness, O have mercy, beloved enemy of my will!
    A Prayer 7

needs
  One positively needs the ease
    The Holy Office 13

negligence
  And many a negligence.
    XXIV 16

neither
  Neither a love where may not be
    XXVII 11
  Neither to malt nor crucifix
    The Holy Office 38

nervous
  And for each maiden, shy and nervous,
    The Holy Office 61

nest
  For there, as in some mossy nest
    XXIII 7

nettles
  Under the moongrey nettles, the black mould
    She Weeps 11

never
  She never seems to think of it;
    The Holy Office 68

never (continued)
My spirit shall they never have
The Holy Office 92

next
This very next lent I will unbare
Gas 91

nigh
And one in fear was standing nigh --
XXX 3

night
Do you hear the night wind and the sighs
III 3
And the night wind answering in antiphon
III 9
Till night is overgone?
III 10
That night allures me where alarms
XXII 9
Thou leanest to the shell of night,
XXVI 1
All day, all night I hear them flowing
XXXV 11
They cry unto the night their battle-name;
XXXVI 5
All night a veil,
Alone 2
The sly reeds whisper to the night
Alone 5
Together, folded by the night, they lay on earth. I hear
A Prayer 14
At night when close in bed she lies
The Holy Office 69
Plays every night at catch-as-catch-can
Gas 81

night-dew
The night-dew lies
XIV 3

night's
Night's sindark nave.
Nightpiece 6
To night's nave upsoaring,
Nightpiece 14

no

O bend no more in revery
IV 7

I read no more,
V 6

Where no rude wind might visit me.
VI 3

No more be tears in moon or mist
XII 11

There is no word nor any sign
XVII 5

Now, O now, we hear no more
XXXIII 13

Is crying "Sleep no more."
XXXIV 8

My heart, have you no wisdom thus to despair?
XXXVI 11

No more, return no more!
Watching 4

No more will the wild wind that passes
Watching 7

Return, no more return.
Watching 8

In a manner no blackamoor printer could bear.
Gas 54

No, ladies, my press shall have no share in
Gas 63

nobleness

Holding to ancient nobleness,
XXI 4

noise

All day I hear the noise of waters
XXXV 1

I hear the noise of many waters
XXXV 9

none

Leave greasy lips their kissing. None
A Memory 10

noon

For Love is at his noon;
XIII 14

At noon of day.
XX 4
XX 14

nor
Nor muse: Who may this singer be
IV 9
There is no word nor any sign
XVII 5
He who hath glory lost, nor hath
XXI 1
Nor have I known a love whose praise
XXVII 9
Nor grieve because our love was gay
XXXIII 5
Nor old heart's wisdom yet to know
Bahnhofstrasse 7
Neither to malt nor crucifix
The Holy Office 38
Nor can they ever be exempt
The Holy Office 77
Nor make my soul with theirs as one
The Holy Office 93

north
From the grey deserts of the north?
XXVI 6
I printed folklore from North and South
Gas 41

nose
(Allow me, ladies, to blow my nose)
Gas 28

not
That will not after,
X 6
For seas and lands shall not divide us
XIII 7
And hear you not the thrushes calling,
XVI 5
Be not sad because all men
XIX 1
Shall we not be as wise as they
XXIII 11
Neither a love where may not be
XXVII 11
Gentle lady, do not sing
XXVIII 1
The leaves - they do not sigh at all
XXXIII 11

Grieve not, sweetheart, for anything --
XXXIII 17
Lies not, stark skin and bone.
A Memory 9
Highhearted youth comes not again
Bahnhofstrasse 6
I dare not withstand the cold touch that I dread.
A Prayer 8
Subduer, do not leave me! Only joy, only anguish,
A Prayer 17
The world that was not
Ecce Puer 11
But I must not accounted be
The Holy Office 23
The "dare not" of sweet maidenhood
The Holy Office 65
Who was it said: Resist not evil?
Gas 85

nothing
Do nothing move.
X 8

now
Now, wind, of your good courtesy
XIII 9
O cool is the valley now
XVI 1
For many a choir is singing now
XVI 3
He is a stranger to me now
XVII 7
Come with me now,
XX 15
Love is aweary now.
XXVIII 8
Welcome to us now at the last
XXX 7
Now, O now, in this brown land
XXXIII 1
Which now is ended in this way.
XXXIII 6
Now, O now, we hear no more
XXXIII 13
Sleep now, O sleep now,
XXXIV 1
A voice crying "Sleep now"
XXXIV 3

now (continued)
My kiss will give peace now
XXXIV 9
Sleep on in peace now,
XXXIV 11
Then as now.
She Weeps 8
Falling as through the silence falleth now
Tutto 7
Wherefore receive now from my lip
The Holy Office 9

nowise
Nowise may trouble us;
XXII 10

nude
Your itch and quailing, nude greed of the flesh.
A Memory 4

numbers
A senile sea numbers each single
On the Beach 3

O
O lonely watcher of the skies,
III 2
O bend no more in revery
IV 7
(O sweet it is and fair it is!)
VI 2
(O soft I knock and soft entreat her!)
VI 7
O, it is for my true love
VIII 13
O, it is for my own true love,
VIII 15
Trembles to starlight. Mine, O Mine!
XII 10
O, hurry over the dark lands
XIII 5
Soon, O soon.
XIII 16
O cool is the valley now
XVI 1
O cool and pleasant is the valley
XVI 7

O Sweetheart, hear you
XVIII 1
O, unto the pine-wood
XX 13
That mood of thine, O timorous,
XXVI 7
Still are you beautiful -- but O,
XXIX 3
O, it was out by Donnycarney
XXXI 1
Went murmuring -- O, happily! --
XXXI 6
O come among the laden trees:
XXXII 2
Now, O now, in this brown land
XXXIII 1
Now, O now, we hear no more
XXXIII 13
Sleep now, O sleep now,
XXXIV 1
O you unquiet heart!
XXXIV 2
O sleep, for the winter
XXXIV 7
O you unquiet heart!
XXXIV 12
O hearts, O sighing grasses,
Watching 5
Dark too our hearts, O love, shall lie and cold
She Weeps 9
Uplift and sway, O golden vine,
Flood 9
Blind me with your dark nearness, O have mercy, beloved enemy of my will!
A Prayer 7
Take me, save me, soothe me, O spare me!
A Prayer 18
O, father forsaken,
Ecce Puer 15
O Ireland my first and only love
Gas 25
O lovely land where the shamrock grows!
Gas 27

oar
Loveward above the glancing oar
Watching 2

odorous
The odorous winds are weaving
XIV 5

off
I carry off their filthy streams
The Holy Office 50

office
Perform my office of Katharsis.
The Holy Office 56

O'Leary
To O'Leary Curtis and John Wyse Power
Gas 52

old
The old piano plays an air,
II 5
Forbearing for old friendship' sake,
XXXIII 4
Nor old heart's wisdom yet to know
Bahnhofstrasse 7
An old man gone.
Ecce Puer 14
Steeled in the school of old Aquinas.
The Holy Office 82

once
Or him who once when snug abed
The Holy Office 43

one
One who is singing by your gate.
IV 4
My dove, my beautiful one,
XIV 1
My dove, my beautiful one!
XIV 8
My fair one, my fair dove,
XIV 15
But one unto him
XVIII 9
That high unconsortable one --
XXI 5
That makes as one thing to the lover
XXIV 13

When one at twilight shyly played
XXX 2
And one in fear was standing nigh --
XXX 3
That had his sweet hours many a one;
XXX 6
A birdless heaven, seadusk, one lone star
Tutto 1
One positively needs the ease
The Holy Office 13
How can one fail to be intense?
The Holy Office 22
One of that mumming company --
The Holy Office 24
To sister mummers one and all
The Holy Office 59
Nor make my soul with theirs as one
The Holy Office 93
Betrayed her own leaders, one by one.
Gas 18
Of one hundred pounds on the estimate
Gas 72

one-handled
And the ashes I'll keep in a one-handled urn.
Gas 88

one's
Ruling one's life by common sense
The Holy Office 21

onions
Shite and onions! Do you think I'll print
Gas 55

only
Where only peace might be my part.
VI 8
Subduer, do not leave me! Only joy, only anguish,
A Prayer 17
O Ireland my first and only love
Gas 25

or
No more be tears in moon or mist
XII 11
Lightly come or lightly go:
XXV 1

or (continued)
In Purchas or in Holinshed.
XXVI 12
Love's breath in you is stale, worded or sung,
A Memory 5
Be piteous or terrible
The Holy Office 12
Or him who sober all the day
The Holy Office 29
Or him whose conduct "seems to own"
The Holy Office 31
Or him who plays the ragged patch
The Holy Office 33
Or him who will his hat unfix
The Holy Office 37
Or him who loves his Master dear --
The Holy Office 41
Or him who drinks his pint in fear
The Holy Office 42
Or him who once when snug abed
The Holy Office 43
I read it a hundred times or so,
Gas 6

Oread
Oread, let thy laughter run,
XXV 4

our
Our piping poets solemnize,
XXVII 10
Nor grieve because our love was gay
XXXIII 5
And all around our loneliness
XXXIII 9
Dark too our hearts, O love, shall lie and cold
She Weeps 9

out
Lean out of the window,
V 1
V 15
Go seek her out all courteously,
XIII 1
I pray you, cease to comb out,
XXIV 9
Comb out your long hair,
XXIV 10

O, it was out by Donnycarney
XXXI 1
They come out of the sea and run shouting by the shore.
XXXVI 10

over
Over the laughing land,
VII 10
Dreams is over --
X 14
O, hurry over the dark lands
XIII 5
When over us the wild winds blow --
XXIX 10
That was over here dressed in Austrian yellow,
Gas 50

overgone
Till night is overgone?
III 10

overhead
From furrow to furrow, while overhead
IX 3

owe
But I owe a duty to Ireland:
Gas 13

own
O, it is for my own true love,
VIII 15
Or him whose conduct "seems to own"
The Holy Office 31
Betrayed her own leaders, one by one.
Gas 18

pagan
Confesses all his pagan past --
The Holy Office 36

pain
I gave him pain,
XVII 2
Ah star of evil! star of pain!
Bahnhofstrasse 5

pale
Pale flowers on his mantle,
I 7
The lamp fills with a pale green glow
II 3
The pale gates of sunrise?
III 5
And where the sky's a pale blue cup
VII 9
The pale dew lies
XIV 13
The pale stars their torches,
Nightpiece 2

paler
Whose soul is sere and paler
A Flower 3

parade
Sydney Parade and Sandymount tram,
Gas 57

pardon
Though (asking your pardon) as for the verse
Gas 39

Parnell's
Flung quicklime into Parnell's eye;
Gas 20

part
Where only peace might be my part.
VI 8

parts
Of an Irish writer in foreign parts.
Gas 4

pass
The young leaves as they pass,
VII 6
Whereto I pass at eve of day,
Bahnhofstrasse 2
Comes to pass.
Ecce Puer 12

passes
Who passes in sunlight
VIII 5

Who passes in the sweet sunlight
VIII 7

How love that passes is enough.
XXVIII 4

No more will the wild wind that passes
Watching 7

past

We were grave lovers. Love is past
XXX 5

Of the dark past
Ecce Puer 1

Confesses all his pagan past --
The Holy Office 36

patch

Or him who plays the ragged patch
The Holy Office 33

Patrick

I printed Patrick What-do-you-Colm:
Gas 44

Paul

And a play on the Word and Holy Paul
Gas 33

peace

Where only peace might be my part.
VI 8

Sweetheart, be at peace again --
XIX 3

My kiss will give peace now
XXXIV 9

Sleep on in peace now,
XXXIV 11

penance

I'll penance do with farts and groans
Gas 89

penitent

My penitent buttocks to the air
Gas 92

per cent

That lives on his property's ten per cent:
Gas 36

perform
   Perform my office of Katharsis.
      The Holy Office 56

peripatetic
   Peripatetic scholarship.
      The Holy Office 10

phrase
   For elegant and antique phrase,
      XXVII 7

piano
   The old piano plays an air,
      II 5

piercing
   Piercing the west,
      Tutto 2

pierstakes
   The crazy pierstakes groan;
      On the Beach 2

pinched
   In the playboy shift that he pinched as swag
      Gas 47

pine-forest
   Where the great pine-forest
      XX 7

pine-wood
   In the dark pine-wood
      XX 1

   O, unto the pine-wood
      XX 13

pint
   Or him who drinks his pint in fear --
      The Holy Office 42

piping
   Our piping poets solemnize,
      XXVII 10

piteous
   Be piteous or terrible
      The Holy Office 12

pity
I pity the poor -- that's why I took
Gas 65

pitying
Proud by my downfall, remembering, pitying,
A Prayer 11

places
But Mammon places under ban
The Holy Office 73
Talk about Irish Names of Places!
Gas 60

play
Awake to hear the sweet harps play
III 7
Play on, invisible harps, unto Love,
III 11
Mixes a naggin in his play --
The Holy Office 30
And a play he wrote (you've read it, I'm sure)
Gas 31
And a play on the Word and Holy Paul
Gas 33

playboy
In the playboy shift that he pinched as swag
Gas 47

played
When one at twilight shyly played
XXX 2

playing
All softly playing,
I 9
Of harps playing unto Love to unclose
III 4

plays
The old piano plays an air,
II 5
Or him who plays the ragged patch
The Holy Office 33
Plays every night at catch-as-catch-can
Gas 81

pleasant
O cool and pleasant is the valley
XVI 7

plenary
Of plenary indulgences.
The Holy Office 14

plenilune
Of Love in ancient plenilune,
XII 3

pluck
Pluck forth your heart, saltblood, a fruit of tears.
A Memory 13

Pluck and devour!
A Memory 14

pluming
Smoke pluming their foreheads.
Tilly 8

plunging
And the thunder of horses plunging, foam about their knees:
XXXVI 2

poems
I printed the poems of Mountainy Mutton
Gas 30

poets
Our piping poets solemnize,
XXVII 10

I printed poets, sad, silly and solemn:
Gas 43

poets'
To hold the poets' grammar-book,
The Holy Office 4

poison-dart
Framed to defy the poison-dart,
XXVII 2

pondering
Pondering the uncomfortable.
The Holy Office 20

poor
I pity the poor -- that's why I took
Gas 65
Poor sister Scotland! Her doom is fell;
Gas 67
The poor and deserving prostitute
Gas 80

poor-dressed
But show to all that poor-dressed be
The Holy Office 39

Pope
For everyone knows the Pope can't belch
Gas 23

porch
In the porch of my printing institute
Gas 79

positively
One positively needs the ease
The Holy Office 13

possessed
I laid those treasures I possessed
XXIII 9

pounds
Of one hundred pounds on the estimate
Gas 72

Power
To O'Leary Curtis and John Wyse Power
Gas 52

prairie
And heard the prairie grasses sighing:
Watching 3

praise
Nor have I known a love whose praise
XXVII 9

pray
I pray you go,
XIII 10

pray (continued)
I pray you, cease to comb out,
XXIV 9
Be mine, I pray, a waxen ear
Simples 9

prayed
Where they have crouched and crawled and prayed
The Holy Office 83

predestined
Gentling her awe as to a soul predestined.
A Prayer 5

prefer
Prefer a lying clamour before you:
XIX 2

preference
His preference for a man of "tone" --
The Holy Office 32

presage
Though thy heart presage thee woe,
XXV 2

press
No, ladies, my press shall have no share in
Gas 63
And sobbing beside my printing press
Gas 93

pretty
With many a pretty air.
XXIV 4
Under a pretty air,
XXIV 12
All fair, with many a pretty air
XXIV 15

prevails
Eastward the gradual dawn prevails
XV 5

print
Shite and onions! Do you think I'll print
Gas 55

printed
I printed it all to the very last word
Gas 9
I printed the poems of Mountainy Mutton
Gas 30
I printed mystical books in dozens:
Gas 37
I printed the table-book of Cousins
Gas 38
I printed folklore from North and South
Gas 41
I printed poets, sad, silly and solemn:
Gas 43
I printed Patrick What-do-you-Colm:
Gas 44
I printed the great John Milicent Synge
Gas 45

printer
In a manner no blackamoor printer could bear.
Gas 54

printing
In the porch of my printing institute
Gas 79
And sobbing beside my printing press
Gas 93

prisoned
Where soul with soul lies prisoned.
XXII 12

prisoner
Gladly were I a prisoner.
XXII 6

property's
That lives on his property's ten per cent:
Gas 36

prostitute
The poor and deserving prostitute
Gas 80

proud
Proud by my downfall, remembering, pitying
A Prayer 11

proudly
Proudly answer to their tears:
XIX 7

proxy
Who safe at ingle-nook, by proxy,
The Holy Office 17

psalm
I'll sing a psalm as I watch it burn
Gas 87

publicly
Whenever publicly we meet
The Holy Office 67

publish
That's why I publish far and wide
Gas 77

Purchas
In Purchas or in Holinshed.
XXVI 12

purge
Through me they purge a bellyful.
The Holy Office 58

put
Put in thy heart, my shyly sweet,
XII 2

quailing
Your itch and quailing, nude greed of the flesh.
A Memory 4

quicklime
Flung quicklime into Parnell's eye;
Gas 20

quiet
And quiet to your heart --
XXXIV 10

quite
My quite illegible railway guide.
Gas 78

radiance
  Of cool sweet dew and radiance mild
    Simples 1

ragged
  Or him who plays the ragged patch
    The Holy Office 33

Rahoon
  Rain on Rahoon falls softly, softly falling,
    She Weeps 1

railway
  My quite illegible railway guide.
    Gas 78

raimented
  How is your beauty raimented!
    XXIX 4

rain
  Rain has fallen all the day.
    XXXII 1
  Rain on Rahoon falls softly, softly falling,
    She Weeps 1
  Ever unanswered and the dark rain falling,
    She Weeps 7
  And muttering rain.
    She Weeps 12

raised
  Raised when she has and shaken
    Nightpiece 11

rapture
  To know the rapture of they heart,
    XXVII 4

rather
  Believe me rather that am wise
    XII 7

read
  I read no more,
    V 6
  And all for some strange name he read
    XXVI 11

read (continued)
I read it a hundred times or so,
Gas 6
And a play he wrote (you've read it, I'm sure)
Gas 31

rebate
Colm can tell you I made a rebate
Gas 71

recall
And some woman's legs that I can't recall,
Gas 34

receive
Wherefore receive now from my lip
The Holy Office 9

red
A rogue in red and yellow dress
XXXIII 7
Urging the cattle along a cold red road,
Tilly 2

red-headed
A red-headed Scotchman to keep my book.
Gas 66

reeds
The sly reeds whisper to the night
Alone 5

reins
Disdaining the reins, with fluttering whips, the charioteers.
XXXVI 4

relent
Soft arms that woo me to relent
XXII 3

relieve
Thus I relieve their timid arses,
The Holy Office 55

rememberest
Rememberest.
Tutto 4

remembering
Why then, remembering those shy
Tutto 9
Proud by my downfall, remembering, pitying
A Prayer 11

render
And I but render and confess
XXVII 5

rent
The darkness of my mind was rent
Gas 11

repine
Sweet lures, repine
Tutto 10

repose
At that hour when all things have repose,
III 1
When all things repose do you alone
III 6

resist
Who was it said: Resist not evil?
Gas 85

rest
Shall have rest.
XVIII 16

return
No more, return no more!
Watching 4
Return, no more return.
Watching 8

reverent
And sign crisscross with reverent thumb
Gas 97

revery
O bend no more in revery
IV 7

Review
I gave him for his Irish Review.
Gas 73

ribbons
With ribbons streaming
X 9

rich
The woods their rich apparel wear --
VIII 14

riches
My hope and all my riches is,
XXIII 2
My hope and all my riches - yes! --
XXIII 5

right
Shall dip his right hand in the urn
Gas 96

ring-around
Dancing a ring-around in glee
IX 2

ripple
Ripple all thy flying hair.
XXV 6

river
Strings by the river where
I 3
There's music along the river
I 5

rivers
Seemed it of rivers rushing forth
XXVI 5

road
Urging the cattle along a cold red road,
Tilly 2

rockvine
The rockvine clusters lift and sway.
Flood 2

rogue
A rogue in red and yellow dress
XXXIII 7

Rome
The leaky barge of the Bishop of Rome
Gas 22

room
I have left my room,
V 10

rose
Frail the white rose and frail are
A Flower 1

rosefrail
Rosefrail and fair -- yet frailest
A Flower 5

round
Her smooth round breast;
XVIII 14

roundelay
The villanelle and roundelay!
XXXIII 14

rude
Where no rude wind might visit me.
VI 3

ruling
Ruling one's life by common sense
The Holy Office 21

run
To run in companies.
VII 4

And run upon the sea
XIII 6

Oread, let thy laughter run,
XXV 4

They come out of the sea and run shouting by the shore.
XXXVI 10

rushing
Seemed it of rivers rushing forth
XXVI 5

ruthless
Lambent and vast and ruthless as is thine
Flood 11

ruthlessly
A waste of waters ruthlessly
Flood 5

sad
Because of sad austerities
VI 4
Be not sad because all men
XIX 1
Sad songs about the end of love;
XXVIII 2
We take sad leave at close of day.
XXXIII 16
Sad as the sea-bird is, when going
XXXV 3
Sad is his voice that calls me, sadly calling,
She Weeps 3
How soft, how sad his voice is ever calling,
She Weeps 6
As his sad heart has lain
She Weeps 10
I printed poets, sad, silly and solemn:
Gas 43

sadder
They are sadder than all tears;
XIX 5

sadly
Sad is his voice that calls me, sadly calling,
She Weeps 3

sadness
Lay aside sadness and sing
XXVIII 3

safe
Who safe at ingle-nook, by proxy,
The Holy Office 17

sage
A sage that is but kith and kin
XII 5

said
And sweet were the words she said to me.
XXXI 4

Who was it said: Resist not evil?
Gas 85

sake
Forbearing for old friendship' sake,
XXXIII 4

salad
Gathers the simple salad leaves.
Simples 4

saltblood
Pluck forth your heart, saltblood, a fruit of tears.
A Memory 13

Sandymount
Sydney Parade and Sandymount tram,
Gas 57

sated
Goldbrown upon the sated flood
Flood 1

save
Take me, save me, soothe me, O spare me!
A Prayer 18
'Tis Irish brains that save from doom
Gas 21

saw
Saw you my true love anywhere?
IX 6
Saw Jesus Christ without his head
The Holy Office 44
And I saw the writer's foul intent.
Gas 12

say
And say I come,
XIII 2

scan
Is his, if thou but scan it well,
XXVI 8

scarlet
My scarlet leaves them white as wool:
The Holy Office 57

scholarship
Peripatetic scholarship.
The Holy Office 10

school
Steeled in the school of old Aquinas.
The Holy Office 82

scorn
Among his foes in scorn and wrath
XXI 3

Scotchman
A red-headed Scotchman to keep my book.
Gas 66

Scotland
Poor sister Scotland! Her doom is fell;
Gas 67

sea
Winds of May, that dance on the sea,
IX 1
And run upon the sea
XIII 6
They come out of the sea and run shouting by the shore.
XXXVI 10
A senile sea numbers each single
On the Beach 3
Grey sea I wrap him warm
On the Beach 6
Where brooding day stares down upon the sea
Flood 7

sea-bird
Sad as the sea-bird is, when going
XXXV 3

seadusk
A birdless heaven, seadusk, one lone star
Tutto 1

seas
For seas and land shall not divide us
XIII 7

secretly
While sweetly, gently, secretly,
XV 9

sedate
Sedate and slow and gay;
II 6

see
Will choose her what you see to mouth upon.
A Memory 11
I wish you could see what tears I weep
Gas 75

seek
Go seek her out all courteously,
XIII 1

seemed
Seemed it of rivers rushing forth
XXVI 5

seems
Or him whose conduct "seems to own"
The Holy Office 31
She never seems to think of it;
The Holy Office 68

self-doomed
I stand, the self-doomed, unafraid,
The Holy Office 84

sell
She cannot find any more Stuarts to sell.
Gas 68

senile
A senile sea numbers each single
On the Beach 3

sense
Ruling one's life by common sense
The Holy Office 21

sent
He sent me a book ten years ago:
Gas 5

sent (continued)
This lovely land that always sent
Gas 15

sentimentalist
For thee, sweet sentimentalist.
XII 12

seraphim
Seraphim,
Nightpiece 7

sere
Whose soul is sere and paler
A Flower 3

service
To service till
Nightpiece 9
I do a similar kind service
The Holy Office 62

servitors
On Mammon's countless servitors
The Holy Office 76

severely
Left me severely in the lurch.
The Holy Office 54

sewer
Make me the sewer of their clique.
The Holy Office 48

shadow
Her shadow on the grass;
VII 8
In deep cool shadow
XX 3

shadowy
The shadowy garden where love is.
XXIX 8
That shadowy beauty in her eyes,
The Holy Office 64

shaken
Raised when she has and shaken
Nightpiece 11

shaking
They come shaking in triumph their long, green hair:
XXXVI 9

shall
For seas and land shall not divide us
XIII 7
My breast shall be your bed.
XIV 12
A man shall have sorrow
XVIII 3
For he shall know then
XVIII 5
Shall have rest.
XVIII 16
Shall we not be as wise as they
XXIII 11
In the grave all love shall sleep:
XXVIII 7
And soon shall love dissolved be
XXIX 9
The ways that we shall go upon.
XXX 8
Of memories shall we depart.
XXXII 6
We two shall wander, hand in hand,
XXXIII 3
Dark too our hearts, O love, shall lie and cold
She Weeps 9
My spirit shall they never have
The Holy Office 92
My soul shall spurn them evermore.
The Holy Office 96
No, ladies, my press shall have no share in
Gas 63
Shall dip his right hand in the urn
Gas 96

shamblings
The shamblings of that motley crew,
The Holy Office 80

shame
A swoon of shame.
Alone 8

shamrock

O lovely land where the shamrock grows!
Gas 27

share

No, ladies, my press shall have no share in
Gas 63

she

She bends upon the yellow keys,
II 7

And sweet were the words she said to me.
XXXI 4

Was the kiss she gave to me.
XXXI 8

When the dear love she yielded with a sigh
Tutto 11

And, gathering, she sings an air:
Simples 7

Raised when she has and shaken
Nightpiece 11

She never seems to think of it;
The Holy Office 68

At night when close in bed she lies
The Holy Office 69

She cannot find any more Stuarts to sell.
Gas 68

shell

Thou leanest to the shell of night,
XXVI 1

she's

Silently she's combing
XXIV 1

And still she's combing her long hair
XXIV 7

shield

To shield me from her childish croon
Simples 10

shielded

And mine a shielded heart for her
Simples 11

shift
In the playboy shift that he pinched as swag
Gas 47

shingle
Wind whines and whines the shingle,
On the Beach 1

ship
When I think of the emigrant train and ship.
Gas 76

shite
Shite and onions! Do you think I'll print
Gas 55

shore
They come out of the sea and run shouting by the shore.
XXXVI 10

shorelamps
The shorelamps in the sleeping lake
Alone 3

should
Lest bards in the attempt should err
The Holy Office 7

shoulder
In troop at his shoulder
X 11
And touch his trembling fineboned shoulder
On the Beach 7

shouting
They come out of the sea and run shouting by the shore.
XXXVI 10

show
But show to all that poor-dressed be
The Holy Office 39
To show you for strictures I don't care a button
Gas 29

shy
Shy thoughts and grave wide eyes and hands
II 9

shy (continued)

When the shy star goes forth in heaven
IV 1

Why then, remembering those shy
Tutto 9

And for each maiden, shy and nervous,
The Holy Office 61

shyly

Put in thy heart, my shyly sweet,
XII 2

When one at twilight shyly played
XXX 2

side

Because your voice was at my side
XVII 1

sigh

Their lives ascend as a continual sigh.
XIX 6

The leaves -- they do not sigh at all
XXXIII 11

When the dear love she yielded with a sigh
Tutto 11

sighing

And heard the prairie grasses sighing:
Watching 3

O hearts, O sighing grasses,
Watching 5

sighs

Do you hear the night wind and the sighs
III 3

A music of sighs:
XIV 6

For lo! the trees are full of sighs
XV 3

sign

That is the sign of maidenhood.
XI 12

There is no word nor any sign
XVII 5

The eyes that mock me sign the way
Bahnofstrasse 1

And sign crisscross with reverent thumb
Gas 97

signals
Grey way whose violet signals are
Bahnhofstrasse 3

signs
The signs that mock me as I go.
Bahnhofstrasse 8

silence
Falling as through the silence falleth now
Tutto 7
The moon a web of silence weaves
Simples 2

silent
Cease, silent love! My doom!
A Prayer 6

silently
Silently she's combing,
XXIV 1
Silently and graciously,
XXIV 3

silk
My conscience is fine as Chinese silk:
Gas 69

silly
I printed poets, sad, silly and solemn:
Gas 43

silvery
In silvery arches spanning the air,
IX 5

similar
I do a similar kind service.
The Holy Office 62

simple
Gathers the simple salad leaves.
Simples 4

simples
Who gathers simples of the moon.
Simples 12

sin
My awful sin I will confess.
Gas 94

sindark
Night's sindark nave.
Nightpiece 6

sing
And sing at her window;
XIII 12
Gentle lady, do not sing
XXVIII 1
Lay aside sadness and sing
XXVIII 3
Sing about the long deep sleep
XXVIII 5
I'll sing a psalm as I watch it burn
Gas 87

singer
Nor muse: Who may this singer be
IV 9

singing
One who is singing by your gate.
IV 4
I heard you singing
V 3
For I heard you singing
V 11
Singing and singing
V 13
Singing: The bridal wind is blowing
XIII 13
For many a choir is singing now
XVI 3

single
A senile sea numbers each single
On the Beach 3

sings
He sings in the hollow:
X 2
He sings the bolder;
X 10
And, gathering, she sings an air:
Simples 7

sinister
Because of the black and sinister arts
Gas 3

sister
My sister, my love.
XIV 10
To sister mummers one and all
The Holy Office 59
Poor sister Scotland! Her doom is fell;
Gas 67

skies
O lonely watcher of the skies,
III 2

skin
Lies not, stark skin and bone.
A Memory 9

sky's
And where the sky's a pale blue cup
VII 9

sleep
But sleep to dreamier sleep be wed
XXII 11
Sing about the long deep sleep
XXVIII 5
In the grave all love shall sleep:
XXVIII 7
Sleep now, O sleep now,
XXXIV 1
A voice crying "Sleep now"
XXXIV 3
O sleep, for the winter
XXXIV 7
Is crying "Sleep no more."
XXXIV 8
Sleep on in peace now,
XXXIV 11

sleep (continued)
I moan in sleep when I hear afar their whirling laughter.
XXXVI 6

sleeping
The shorelamps in the sleeping lake
Alone 3
A child is sleeping:
Ecce Puer 13

slimesilvered
Slimesilvered stone.
On the Beach 4

slow
Sedate and slow and gay;
II 6
My slow life! Bend deeper on me, threatening head,
A Prayer 10

slowly
My love goes slowly, bending to
VII 7

slumber
From love's deep slumber and from death,
XV 2

sly
The sly reeds whisper to the night
Alone 5

smoke
Smoke pluming their foreheads.
Tilly 8

smooth
Her smooth round breast;
XVIII 14

snood
The snood upon thy yellow hair.
XI 6
And softly to undo the snood
XI 11

snug
Or him who once when snug abed
The Holy Office 43

so
So I were ever in that heart.
VI 10
With mien so virginal?
VIII 8
Carry so brave attire?
VIII 12
That is so young and fair.
VIII 16
So he who has sorrow
XVIII 15
Of that so sweet imprisonment
XXII 1
Ever so little falsity.
XXVII 12
Lightly, lightly -- ever so:
XXV 7
Dear heart, why will you use me so?
XXIX 1
Alas! why will you use me so?
XXIX 12
Where love did so sweet music make
XXXIII 2
As thou, fond heart, love's time, so faint, so far,
Tutto 3
And tried so hard to win for us
The Holy Office 45
So distantly I turn to view
The Holy Office 79
I read it a hundred times or so,
Gas 6
So gross a libel on Stepmother Erin.
Gas 64
I'll burn that book, so help me devil.
Gas 86

soaring
Arches on soaring arches,
Nightpiece 5

soars
Who soars above on an angel's wing
Gas 46

sobbing
And sobbing beside my printing press
Gas 93

sober
Or him who sober all the day
The Holy Office 29

soft
At that hour when soft lights come and go,
III 13
Soft sweet music in the air above
III 14
(O soft I knock and soft entreat her!)
VI 7
Gleam with a soft and golden fire --
VIII 10
With a soft tumult
XX 11
Soft arms that woo me to relent
XXII 3
In that soft choiring of delight
XXVI 3
Through the soft cry of kiss to kiss,
XXIX 6
How soft, how sad his voice is ever calling,
She Weeps 6
The clear young eyes' soft look, the candid brow,
Tutto 5
Knows the soft flame that is desire.
The Holy Office 72
My heart is as soft as buttermilk.
Gas 70

softer
His song is softer than the dew
IV 5
But softer than the breath of summer
XXXI 7

softly
All softly playing,
I 9
Begin thou softly to unzone
XI 9
And softly to undo the snood
XI 11

Will softly move
XVIII 10

And softly woo him
XVIII 11

Rain on Rahoon falls softly, softly falling,
She Weeps 1

softly-burning

Where softly-burning fires appear,
XV 6

solemn

I printed poets, sad, silly and solemn:
Gas 43

solemnize

Our piping poets solemnize,
XXVII 10

some

For there, as in some mossy nest
XXIII 7

And all for some strange name he read
XXVI 11

And some woman's legs that I can't recall,
Gas 34

sometime

Where love did sometime go.
XVI 4

son

Forgive your son!
Ecce Puer 16

song

His song is softer than the dew
IV 5

Whose song about my heart is falling?
IV 10

That song and laughter
X 7

Wind of spices whose song is ever
XIII 3

song-confessed

Love and laughter song-confessed
XXV 11

songs
Sad songs about the end of love;
XXVIII 2

soon
And soon will your true love be with you,
XIII 15
Soon, O soon.
XIII 16
And soon shall love dissolved be
XXIX 9

soothe
Take me, save me, soothe me, O spare me!
A Prayer 18

sorrow
A man shall have sorrow
XVIII 3
So he who has sorrow
XVIII 15

soul
From dewy dreams, my soul, arise,
XV 1
Found any soul to fellow his,
XXI 2
My soul, dearest, is fain --
XXII 2
Where soul with soul lies prisoned.
XXII 12
Whose soul is sere and paler
A Flower 3
And all my soul is a delight,
Alone 7
Gentling her awe as to a soul predestined.
A Prayer 5
Nor make my soul with theirs as one
The Holy Office 93
My soul shall spurn them evermore.
The Holy Office 96
It's a wonder to me, upon my soul,
Gas 61

souls
Waste of souls.
Nightpiece 18

Those souls that hate the strength that mine has
The Holy Office 81

sound
What sound hath made thy heart to fear?
XXVI 4

sour
As sour as cat's breath,
A Memory 6

South
I printed folklore from North and South
Gas 41

spanning
In silvery arches spanning the air,
IX 5

spare
Take me, save me, soothe me, O spare me!
A Prayer 18

speak
Speak to your heart.
XXXII 8
But all these men of whom I speak
The Holy Office 47

spices
Wind of spices whose song is ever
XIII 3

spirit
And that high spirit ever wars
The Holy Office 75
My spirit shall they never have
The Holy Office 92
And in a spirit of Irish fun
Gas 17

spouting
Spouting Italian by the hour
Gas 51

springtide
With springtide all adorning her?
VIII 2

spurn
And though they spurn me from their door
The Holy Office 95
My soul shall spurn them evermore.
The Holy Office 96

stale
Love's breath in you is stale, worded or sung,
A Memory 5

stand
Arrogant, in black armour, behind them stand,
XXXVI 3
I stand, the self-doomed, unafraid,
The Holy Office 84

standing
And one in fear was standing nigh --
XXX 3

star
When the shy star goes forth in heaven
IV 1
A birdless heaven, seadusk, one lone star
Tutto 1
The trysting and the twining star.
Bahnhofstrasse 4
Ah star of evil! star of pain!
Bahnhofstrasse 5

stares
Where brooding day stares down upon the sea
Flood 7
This grey that stares
A Memory 8

stark
Lies not, stark skin and bone.
A Memory 9

starknell
A starknell tolls
Nightpiece 15

starlight
Trembles to starlight. Mine, O Mine!
XII 10

stars
Glory and stars beneath his feet --
XII 4
A moondew stars her hanging hair
Simples 5
The pale stars their torches,
Nightpiece 2

stay
There, where the gay winds stay to woo
VII 5
And there, love, will we stay.
XVI 8

staying
Staying and going hence,
XXIV 14
Staying a little by the way
XXXII 5

steeled
Steeled in the school of old Aquinas.
The Holy Office 82

stepmother
So gross a libel on Stepmother Erin.
Gas 64

still
And still she's combing her long hair
XXIV 7
Still are you beautiful -- but O,
XXIX 3
In the still garden where a child
Simples 3
Draw from me still
A Prayer 9

stirred
The flowery bells of morn are stirred
XV 10

stone
Slimesilvered stone.
On the Beach 4

strange
And all for some strange name he read
XXVI 11

stranger
He is a stranger to me now
XVII 7

straying
And fingers straying
I 11

stream
I bleed by the black stream
Tilly 11

streamers
Bright cap and streamers,
X 1

streaming
With ribbons streaming
X 9

streams
I carry off their filthy streams
The Holy Office 50

strength
Come, give, yield all your strength to me!
A Prayer 2
Those souls that hate the strength that mine has
The Holy Office 81

stretch
Tonight stretch full by the fire!
Tilly 10

strictures
To show you for strictures I don't care a button
Gas 29

strings
Strings in the earth and air
I 1
Strings by the river where
I 3

Stuarts
She cannot find any more Stuarts to sell.
Gas 68

subduer
Subduer, do not leave me! Only joy, only anguish,
A Prayer 17

submission's
Its cruel calm, submission's misery,
A Prayer 4

sullen
Of sullen day.
Flood 4

summer
Along with us the summer wind
XXXI 5
But softer than the breath of summer
XXXI 7

sun
The sun is in the willow leaves
XXIV 5
Vales and many a wasted sun,
XXV 3
He travels after a winter sun,
Tilly 1

sung
Love's breath in you is stale, worded or sung,
A Memory 5

sunlight
Who passes in the sunlight
VIII 5
Who passes in the sweet sunlight
VIII 7

sunny
For whom does all the sunny woodland
VIII 11

sunrise
The pale gates of sunrise?
III 5

sure
And a play he wrote (you've read it, I'm sure)
Gas 31

surges

As the bleak incense surges, cloud on cloud,
Nightpiece 16

surprise

For I detect without surprise
The Holy Office 63

swag

In the playboy shift that he pinched as swag
Gas 47

sway

The rockvine clusters lift and sway.
Flood 2

Uplift and sway, O golden vine,
Flood 9

sways

Sways and uplifts its weedy mane
Flood 6

Sweet

Make music sweet;
I 2

Awake to hear the sweet harps play
III 7

Soft sweet music in the air above
III 14

I would in that sweet bosom be
VI 1

I would in the sweet bosom be
VI 5

(O sweet it is and fair it is!)
VI 2

Who passes in the sweet sunlight
VIII 7

Put in thy heart, my shyly sweet,
XII 2

For thee, sweet sentimentalist.
XII 12

How sweet to lie there,
XX 5

Sweet to kiss,
XX 6

Sweet love, away.
XX 16

Of that so sweet imprisonment
XXII 1
That had his sweet hours many a one;
XXX 6
And sweet were the words she said to me.
XXXI 4
Where Love did so sweet music make
XXXIII 2
Sweet lures, repine
Tutto 10
Of cool sweet dew and radiance mild
Simples 1
The "dare not" of sweet maidenhood
The Holy Office 65

sweeter
Austerities were all the sweeter
VI 9
Sweeter were
XX 10

sweetheart
Sweetheart, I come.
X 16
O Sweetheart, hear you
XVIII 1
Sweetheart, be at peace again --
XIX 3
Yet will we kiss, sweetheart, before
XXXIII 15
XXXIII 17

sweetly
While sweetly, gently, secretly,
XV 9

swoon
A swoon of shame.
Alone 8

Sydney
Sydney Parade and Sandymount tram,
Gas 57

Synge
I printed the great John Milicent Synge
Gas 45

table
  Like him who finds a joy at table
    The Holy Office 19

table-book
  I printed the table-book of Cousins
    Gas 38

take
  We take sad leave at close of day.
    XXXIII 16
  Take me, save me, soothe me, O spare me!
    A Prayer 18

takes
  When the year takes them in the fall.
    XXXIII 12

tale
  Your lover's tale;
    XVIII 2
  Who a mad tale bequeaths to us
    XXVI 9

talk
  Where they talk of "bastard," "bugger" and "whore,"
    Gas 32
  Talk about Irish Names of Places!
    Gas 60

tavern
  Bringing to tavern and to brothel
    The Holy Office 5

taxation
  From his taxation of contempt.
    The Holy Office 78

tears
  No more be tears in moon or mist
    XII 11
  They are sadder than all tears;
    XIX 5
  Proudly answer to their tears:
    XIX 7
  Pluck forth your heart, saltblood, a fruit of tears.
    A Memory 13

I wish you could see what tears I weep
Gas 75

teeth
The thirteen teeth
A Memory 2

telescope
Through both the ends of a telescope.
Gas 8

tell
Colm can tell you I made a rebate
Gas 71

tells
The voice tells them home is warm.
Tilly 5

ten
He sent me a book ten years ago:
Gas 5
That lives on his property's ten percent:
Gas 36

tenderness
The malice of thy tenderness.
XXVII 6

tendrils
Laburnum tendrils trail.
Alone 4

terrible
Be piteous or terrible
The Holy Office 12

than
His song is softer than the dew
IV 5
They are sadder than all tears;
XIX 5
But softer than the breath of summer
XXXI 7
Than time's wan wave.
A Flower 4

that
That wander as they list --
II 10
At that hour when all things have repose,
III 1
At that hour when soft lights come and go,
III 13
'Tis I that am your visitant.
IV 12
I would in that sweet bosom be
VI 1
VI 5
I would be ever in that heart
VI 6
So I were ever in that heart.
VI 10
By ways that know the light footfall?
VIII 6
That is so young and fair.
VIII 16
Winds of May, that dance on the sea,
IX 1
All you that love.
X 4
That will not after,
X 6
That song and laughter
X 7
The zone that doth become thee fair,
XI 5
That is the sign of maidenhood.
XI 12
A sage that is but kith and kin
XII 5
Believe me rather that am wise
XII 7
That high unconsortable one --
XXI 5
Of that so sweet imprisonment
XXII 1
Soft arms that woo me to relent
XXII 3
That night allures me where alarms
XXII 9
This heart that flutters near my heart
XXIII 1
Ere that mine eyes had learned to weep.
XXIII 10

That makes as one thing to the lover
XXIV 13
Clouds that wrap the vales below
XXV 8
In that soft choiring of delight
XXVI 3
That mood of thine, O timorous,
XXVI 7
How love that passes is enough.
XXVIII 4
Of lovers that are dead, and how
XXVIII 6
Dear eyes that gently me upbraid,
XXIX 2
That had his sweet hours many a one;
XXX 6
The ways that we shall go upon.
XXX 8
No more will the wild wind that passes
Watching 7
Her hands that gave
A Flower 2
Sad is his voice that calls me, sadly calling,
She Weeps 3
This grey that stares
A Memory 8
The eyes that mock me sign the way
Bahnhofstrasse 1
The signs that mock me as I go.
Bahnhofstrasse 8
I dare not withstand the cold touch that I dread.
A Prayer 8
The world that was not
Ecce Puer 11
One of that mumming company --
The Holy Office 24
But show to all that poor-dressed be
The Holy Office 39
That they may dream their dreamy dreams
The Holy Office 49
That shadowy beauty in her eyes,
The Holy Office 64
That answers my corruptive "would."
The Holy Office 66
Knows the soft flame that is desire.
The Holy Office 72
And that high spirit ever wars
The Holy Office 75

that (continued)
The shamblings of that motley crew,
The Holy Office 80
Those souls that hate the strength that mine has
The Holy Office 81
This lovely land that always sent
Gas 15
'Tis Irish brains that save from doom
Gas 21
And some woman's legs that I can't recall,
Gas 34
That lives on his property's ten per cent:
Gas 36
In the playboy shift that he pinched as swag
Gas 47
But I draw the line at that bloody fellow
Gas 49
That was over here dressed in Austrian yellow,
Gas 50
I'll burn that book, so help me devil.
Gas 86

that's
I pity the poor -- that's why I took
Gas 65
That's why I publish far and wide
Gas 77

thee
Thee and woo thy girlish ways --
XI 4
The zone that doth become thee fair,
XI 5
For thee, sweet sentimentalist.
XII 12
Though thy heart presage thee woe,
XXV 2

their
The woods their rich apparel wear --
VIII 14
Their lives ascend as a continual sigh.
XIX 6
Proudly answer to their tears:
XIX 7
Their words come to.
XVIII 8

And the thunder of horses plunging, foam about their knees:
XXXVI 2
They cry unto the night their battle-name:
XXXVI 5
I moan in sleep when I hear afar their whirling laughter.
XXXVI 6
They come shaking in triumph their long, green hair:
XXXVI 9
They moo and make brute music with their hoofs.
Tilly 6
Smoke pluming their foreheads.
Tilly 8
I heard their young hearts crying
Watching 1
The pale stars their torches,
Nightpiece 2
Leave greasy lips their kissing. None
A Memory 10
Make me the sewer of their clique.
The Holy Office 48
That they may dream their dreamy dreams
The Holy Office 49
I carry off their filthy streams
The Holy Office 50
Thus I relieve their timid arses,
The Holy Office 55
And though they spurn me from their door
The Holy Office 95

theirs
Nor make my soul with theirs as one
The Holy Office 93

them
When the year takes them in the fall.
XXXIII 12
All day, all night, I hear them flowing
XXXV 11
Arrogant, in black armour, behind them stand,
XXXVI 3
Calling to them, a voice they know,
Tilly 3
The voice tells them home is warm.
Tilly 5
He drives them with a flowering branch before him,
Tilly 7

them (continued)
For I can do those things for them
The Holy Office 51
My scarlet leaves them white as wool:
The Holy Office 57
Let them continue as is meet
The Holy Office 89
My soul shall spurn them evermore.
The Holy Office 96

then
For he shall know then
XVIII 5
Then as now.
She Weeps 8
Why then, remembering those shy
Tutto 9

there
For love wanders there,
I 6
There, where the gay winds stay to woo
VII 5
And there, love, will we go
XVI 2
And there, love, will we stay.
XVI 8
There is no word nor any sign
XVII 5
How sweet to lie there,
XX 5
Ah, could they ever hold me there
XXII 5
For there, as in some mossy nest
XXIII 7

there's
There's music along the river
I 5

these
But all these men of whom I speak
The Holy Office 47

they
That wander as they list --
II 10

The young leaves as they pass,
VII 6
Can they dishonour you?
XIX 4
They are sadder than all tears;
XIX 5
As they deny, deny.
XIX 8
Ah, could they ever hold me there
XXII 5
Shall we not be as wise as they
XXIII 11
The leaves -- they do not sigh at all
XXXIII 11
They cry unto the night their battle-name:
XXXVI 5
They cleave the gloom of dreams, a blinding flame,
XXXVI 7
They come shaking in triumph their long, green hair:
XXXVI 9
They come out of the sea and run shouting by the shore.
XXXVI 10
Calling to them, a voice they know,
Tilly 3
They moo and make brute music with their hoofs.
Tilly 6
They mouth love's language. Gnash
A Memory 1
Together, folded by the night, they lay on earth. I hear
A Prayer 14
While they console him when he whinges
The Holy Office 27
That they may dream their dreamy dreams
The Holy Office 49
Through me they purge a bellyful.
The Holy Office 58
Nor can they ever be exempt
The Holy Office 77
Where they have crouched and crawled and prayed
The Holy Office 83
Though they may labour to the grave
The Holy Office 91
My spirit shall they never have
The Holy Office 92
And though they spurn me from their door
The Holy Office 95
Where they talk of "*bastard*," "*bugger*" and "*whore*,"
Gas 32

thick
The leaves lie thick upon the way
XXXII 3

thighs
And feels my hand between her thighs
The Holy Office 70

thine
That mood of thine, O timorous,
XXVI 7

Was all but thine?
Tutto 12

Lambent and vast and ruthless as is thine
Flood 11

thing
That makes as one thing to the lover
XXIV 13

things
At that hour when all things have repose,
III 1

When all things repose do you alone
III 6

For I can do those things for them
The Holy Office 51

Those things for which Grandmother Church
The Holy Office 53

thirteen
The thirteen teeth
A Memory 2

think
She never seems to think of it;
The Holy Office 68

Shite and onions! Do you think I'll print
Gas 55

When I think of the emigrant train and ship.
Gas 76

this
Her head inclines this way.
II 8

Nor muse: Who may this singer be
IV 9

Know you by this, the lover's chant,
IV 11
This heart that flutters near my heart
XXIII 1
Now, O now, in this brown land
XXXIII 1
Which now is ended in this way.
XXXIII 6
This grey that stares
A Memory 8
This name, Katharsis-Purgative.
The Holy Office 2
This lovely land that always sent
Gas 15
This very next lent I will unbare
Gas 91

those
A glory kindles in those eyes,
XII 9
Making to tremble all those veils
XV 7
I laid those treasures I possessed
XXIII 9
Why then, remembering those shy
Tutto 9
For I can do those things for them
The Holy Office 51
Those things for which Grandmother Church
The Holy Office 53
Those souls that hate the strength that mine has
The Holy Office 81

thou
When thou has heard his name upon
XI 7
Begin thou softly to unzone
XI 9
Thou leanest to the shell of night,
XXVI 1
Is his, if thou but scan it well,
XXVI 8
Yet must thou fold me unaware
XXVII 3
In gentle eyes thou veilest,
A Flower 7
Love, hear thou
She Weeps 5

thou (continued)
As thou, fond heart, love's time, so faint, so far,
Tutto 3
Fair as the wave is, fair, art thou!
Simples 8

though
Though love live but a day?
XXIII 12
Though thy heart presage thee woe,
XXV 2
Though I thy Mithridates were,
XXVII 1
Though they may labour to the grave
The Holy Office 91
And though they spurn me from their door
The Holy Office 95
Though (asking your pardon) as for the verse
Gas 39

thoughts
Shy thoughts and grave wide eyes and hands
II 9

threatening
My slow life! Bend deeper on me, threatening head,
A Prayer 10

through
Through the gloom.
V 12
Dearest, through interwoven arms
XXII 7
Through the clear mirror of your eyes,
XXIX 5
Through the soft cry of kiss to kiss,
XXIX 6
Falling as through the silence falleth now
Tutto 7
Through which I lost my diadem,
The Holy Office 52
Through me they purge a bellyful.
The Holy Office 58
Through both the ends of a telescope.
Gas 8

thrushes
And hear you not the thrushes calling,
XVI 5

thumb
And sign crisscross with reverent thumb
Gas 97

thunder
And the thunder of horses plunging, foam about their knees:
XXXVI 2

thurible
Her thurible.
Nightpiece 12

thus
My heart, have you no wisdom thus to despair?
XXXVI 11
Thus I relieve their timid arses,
The Holy Office 55

thy
Thee and woo thy girlish ways --
XI 4
The snood upon thy yellow hair.
XI 6
Thy girlish bosom unto him
XI 10
Put in thy heart, my shyly sweet,
XII 2
Thy kiss descending
XX 9
Of thy hair.
XX 12
Though thy heart presage thee woe,
XXV 2
Oread, let thy laughter run,
XXV 4
Ripple all thy flying hair.
XXV 6
What sound hath made thy heart to fear?
XXVI 4
Though I thy Mithridates were,
XXVII 1
To know the rapture of thy heart,
XXVII 4
The malice of thy tenderness.
XXVII 6

tight-breeched
    With her tight-breeched British artilleryman
                                        Gas 82

till
    Till night is overgone?
                                        III 10
    Till the irreverent mountain air
                                        XXV 5
    To service till
                                        Nightpiece 9
    Till the Mahamanvantara be done:
                                        The Holy Office 94

time
    And the time of dreaming
                                        X 13
    Love came to us in time gone by
                                        XXX 1
    As thou, fond heart, love's time, so faint, so far,
                                        Tutto 3

times
    I read it a hundred times or so,
                                        Gas 6

time's
    Than time's wan wave.
                                        A Flower 4

timid
    Thus I relieve their timid arses,
                                        The Holy Office 55

timorous
    That mood of thine, O timorous,
                                        XXVI 7

'Tis
    'Tis I that am your visitant.
                                        IV 12
    'Tis Irish brains that save from doom
                                        Gas 21

together
    My love and I did walk together;
                                        XXXI 3

Together, folded by the night, they lay on earth. I hear
A Prayer 14

tolls
A starknell tolls
Nightpiece 15

tone
His preference for a man of "tone" --
The Holy Office 32

tongue
Harsh of tongue.
A Memory 7

tonight
Tonight stretch full by the fire!
Tilly 10

too
Dearest, my lips wax all too wise;
XXVII 8
But you, dear love, too dear to me,
XXIX 11
Dark too our hearts, O love, shall lie and cold
She Weeps 9

took
I pity the poor -- that's why I took
Gas 65

torches
The pale stars their torches,
Nightpiece 2

torn
For my torn bough!
Tilly 12
My heart is torn.
Ecce Puer 4

touch
And touch his trembling fineboned shoulder
On the Beach 7
I dare not withstand the cold touch that I dread.
A Prayer 8

trail
Laburnum tendrils trail.
Alone 4

train
When I think of the emigrant train and ship.
Gas 76

tram
Sydney Parade and Sandymount tram,
Gas 57

travel
To enter heaven, travel hell,
The Holy Office 11

travelling
From Maunsel's manager's travelling bag.
Gas 48

travels
He travels after a winter sun,
Tilly 1

treasures
The wrens will divers treasures keep,
XXIII 8
I laid those treasures I possessed
XXIII 9

tree
I wait by the cedar tree,
XIV 9
When the bat flew from tree to tree
XXXI 2
Is knocking, knocking at the tree;
XXXIII 8

trees
The trees of the avenue.
II 4
For lo! the trees are full of sighs
XV 3
O come among the laden trees:
XXXII 2

tremble
Making to tremble all those veils
XV 7

trembled
To hear why earth and heaven trembled
Gas 2

trembles
Trembles to starlight. Mine, O Mine!
XII 10

trembling
And touch his trembling fineboned shoulder
On the Beach 7

tremulous
By love made tremulous,
XXII 8

tried
And tried so hard to win for us
The Holy Office 45

triumph
They come shaking in triumph their long, green hair:
XXXVI 9

troop
In troop at his shoulder
X 11

trouble
Nowise may trouble us;
XXII 10

true
O, it is for my true love
VIII 13
O, it is for my own true love,
VIII 15
Saw you my true love anywhere?
IX 6
And soon will your true love be with you,
XIII 15

true-born
For every true-born mysticist
The Holy Office 15

trysting
The trysting and the twining star.
Bahnhofstrasse 4

tumult
With a soft tumult
XX 11

turn
So distantly I turn to view
The Holy Office 79

turns
The twilight turns from amethyst
II 1
The twilight turns to darker blue
II 11

'Twas
'Twas Irish humour, wet and dry,
Gas 19

twilight
The twilight turns from amethyst
II 1
The twilight turns to darker blue
II 11
When one at twilight shyly played
XXX 2

twining
The trysting and the twining star.
Bahnhofstrasse 4

two
We two shall wander, hand in hand,
XXXIII 3

'Twould
'Twould give you a heartburn on your arse:
Gas 40

unafraid
I stand, the self-doomed, unafraid,
The Holy Office 84

unanswered
Ever unanswered and the dark rain falling,
She Weeps 7

unaware

Yet must thou fold me unaware

XXVII 3

unbare

This very next lent I will unbare

Gas 91

unclose

Of harps playing unto Love to unclose

III 4

Unclose his eyes!

Ecce Puer 8

uncomfortable

Pondering the uncomfortable.

The Holy Office 20

unconsortable

That high unconsortable one --

XXI 5

under

His hand is under

XVIII 13

Under a pretty air,

XXIV 12

Under the moongrey nettles, the black mould

She Weeps 11

But Mammon places under ban

The Holy Office 73

undo

And softly to undo the snood

XI 11

unending

And in my heart how deep unending

On the Beach 11

unfellowed

Unfellowed, friendless and alone,

The Holy Office 85

unfix

Or him who will his hat unfix

The Holy Office 37

unhappy
Love is unhappy when love is away!
IX 9
Unhappy when we draw apart
XXIII 3

unprejudiced
A Dante is, unprejudiced
The Holy Office 16

unquiet
O you unquiet heart!
XXXIV 2
XXXIV 12

unto
Of harps playing unto Love to unclose
III 4
Play on, invisible harps, unto Love,
III 11
Thy girlish bosom unto him
XI 10
But one unto him
XVIII 9
O, unto the pine-wood
XX 13
They cry unto the night their battle-name:
XXXVI 5
Myself unto myself will give
The Holy Office 1

untrue
Friends be untrue
XVIII 6

unzone
Begin thou softly to unzone
XI 9

up
My love goes lightly, holding up
VII 11
The foam flies up to be garlanded,
IX 4
Backwards and forwards, down and up,
Gas 7

upbraid
Dear eyes that gently me upbraid,
XXIX 2

uplift
Uplift and sway, O golden vine,
Flood 9

uplifts
Sways and uplifts its weedy mane
Flood 6

upon
Upon an instrument.
I 12
She bends upon the yellow keys,
II 7
The snood upon thy yellow hair.
XI 6
When thou hast heard his name upon
XI 7
And run upon the sea
XIII 6
Upon my lips and eyes.
XIV 4
The ways that we shall go upon.
XXX 8
The leaves lie thick upon the way
XXXII 3
I hear an army charging upon the land,
XXXVI 1
Clanging, clanging upon the heart as upon an anvil.
XXXVI 8
Goldbrown upon the sated flood
Flood 1
Where brooding day stares down upon the sea
Flood 7
Will choose her what you see to mouth upon.
A Memory 11
Come! I yield. Bend deeper upon me! I am here.
A Prayer 16
It's a wonder to me, upon my soul,
Gas 61
Kneeling upon my marrowbones.
Gas 90
Memento homo upon my bum.
Gas 98

upsoaring
To night's nave upsoaring,
Nightpiece 14

urging
Urging the cattle along a cold red road,
Tilly 2

urn
And the ashes I'll keep in a one-handled urn.
Gas 88
Shall dip his right hand in the urn
Gas 96

us
For seas and land shall not divide us
XIII 7
Calling us away?
XVI 6
Nowise may trouble us;
XXII 10
Who a mad tale bequeaths to us
XXVI 9
When over us the wild winds blow --
XXIX 10
Love came to us in time gone by
XXX 1
Welcome to us now at the last
XXX 7
Along with us the summer wind
XXXI 5
Around us fear, descending
On the Beach 9
And tried so hard to wind for us
The Holy Office 45

use
Dear heart, why will you use me so?
XXIX 1
Alas! why will you use me so?
XXIX 12

uses
The uses of Leviathan
The Holy Office 74

vainly
Vainly your loveblown bannerets mourn!
Watching 6

vales
Vales and many a wasted sun,
XXV 3
Clouds that wrap the vales below
XXV 8

valley
O cool is the valley now
XVI 1
O cool and pleasant is the valley
XVI 7

vast
Vast wings above the lambent waters brood
Flood 3
Lambent and vast and ruthless as is thine
Flood 11

veil
Like a veil on my head.
XIV 14
All night a veil,
Alone 2

veilest
In gentle eyes thou veilest,
A Flower 7

veils
Making to tremble all those veils
XV 7

verges
Ghostfires from heaven's far verges faint illume,
Nightpiece 4

verse
Though (asking your pardon) as for the verse
Gas 39

very
I printed it all to the very last word
Gas 9

very (continued)
This very next lent I will unbare
Gas 91

vicar-general
I act as vicar-general
The Holy Office 60

view
So distantly I turn to view
The Holy Office 79

villanelle
The villanelle and roundelay!
XXXIII 14

vine
Uplift and sway, O golden vine,
Flood 9

violet
Grey way whose violet signals are
Bahnhofstrasse 3

virginal
With mien so virginal?
VIII 8

visit
And he is come to visit you.
IV 6

Where no rude wind might visit me.
VI 3

visitant
'Tis I that am your visitant.
IV 12

voice
Because your voice was at my side
XVII 1

A voice crying "Sleep now"
XXXIV 3

The voice of the winter
XXXIV 5

Calling to them, a voice they know,
Tilly 3

The voice tells them home is warm.
Tilly 5
Sad is his voice that calls me, sadly calling,
She Weeps 3
How soft, how sad his voice is ever calling,
She Weeps 6

voidward
Voidward from the adoring
Nightpiece 17

wait
I wait by the cedar tree,
XIV 9

walk
My love and I did walk together;
XXXI 3

Walsh
Without the consent of Billy Walsh.
Gas 24

wan
Than time's wan wave.
A Flower 4

wander
That wander as they list --
II 10
We two shall wander, hand in hand,
XXXIII 3

wanders
For Love wanders there,
I 6

warm
The voice tells them home is warm.
Tilly 5
Grey sea I wrap him warm
On the Beach 6

wars
And that high spirit ever wars
The Holy Office 75

was

My book was closed;
V 5

Because your voice was at my side
XVII 1

Who was my friend.
XVII 8

And one in fear was standing nigh --
XXX 3

O, it was out by Donnycarney
XXXI 1

Was the kiss she gave to me.
XXXI 8

Nor grieve because our love was gay
XXXIII 5

Was all but thine?
Tutto 12

Him who is, him who was!
A Prayer 12

The world that was not
Ecce Puer 11

The darkness of my mind was rent
Gas 11

That was over here dressed in Austrian yellow,
Gas 50

Who was it said: Resist not evil?
Gas 85

waste

A waste of waters ruthlessly
Flood 5

Waste of souls.
Nightpiece 18

wasted

Vales and many a wasted sun,
XXV 3

watch

I'll sing a psalm as I watch it burn
Gas 87

watcher

O lonely watcher of the skies,
III 2

watching

Watching the fire dance
V 7

waters
All day I hear the noise of waters
XXXV 1
He hears the winds cry to the waters'
XXXV 5
I hear the noise of many waters
XXXV 9
Vast wings above the lambent waters brood
Flood 3
A waste of waters ruthlessly
Flood 5

wave
Than time's wan wave.
A Flower 4
Fair as the wave is, fair, art thou!
Simples 8
Enshrouded, wave.
Nightpiece 3

wax
Dearest, my lips wax all too wise;
XXVII 8

waxen
Be mine, I pray, a waxen ear
Simples 9

way
Her head inclines this way.
II 8
To Love before him on his way,
III 8
Whose way in heaven is aglow
III 12
The leaves lie thick upon the way
XXXII 3
Staying a little by the way
XXXII 5
Which now is ended in this way.
XXXIII 6
The eyes that mock me sign the way
Bahnhofstrasse 1
Grey way whose violet signals are
Bahnhofstrasse 3

ways

By ways that know the light footfall?
VIII 6

The ways of all the woodland
VIII 9

In ways of love.
XVIII 12

Thee and woo thy girlish ways --
XI 4

The ways that we shall go upon.
XXX 8

I, who dishevelled ways forsook
The Holy Office 3

we

And there, love, will we go
XVI 2

And there, love, will we stay.
XVI 8

I would we lay,
XX 2

Unhappy when we draw apart
XXIII 3

Shall we not be as wise as they
XXIII 11

We were grave lovers. Love is past
XXX 5

The ways that we shall go upon.
XXX 8

Of memories shall we depart.
XXXII 6

We two shall wander, hand in hand,
XXXIII 3

Now, O now, we hear no more
XXXIII 13

Yet will we kiss, sweetheart, before
XXXIII 15

We take sad leave at close of day.
XXXIII 16

Whenever publicly we meet
The Holy Office 67

wear

The woods their rich apparel wear --
VIII 14

weaves
The moon a web of silence weaves
Simples 2

weaving
The odorous winds are weaving
XIV 5

web
The moon a web of silence weaves
Simples 2

wed
But sleep to dreamier sleep be wed
XXII 11

weedy
Sways and uplifts its weedy mane
Flood 6

weep
Ere that mine eyes had learned to weep.
XXIII 10
I wish you could see what tears I weep
Gas 75

weeping
But weeping after holy fast
The Holy Office 35

welcome
Welcome to us now at the last
XXX 7

well
Is his, if thou but scan it well,
XXVI 8

Welladay
Welladay! Welladay!
IX 7

Wellington
The name of the Wellington Monument,
Gas 56

went
  Went murmuring -- O, happily! --
XXXI 6

were
  Austerities were all the sweeter
VI 9
  So I were ever in that heart.
VI 10
  Sweeter were
XX 10
  Gladly were I a prisoner!
XXII 6
  Though I thy Mithridates were,
XXVII 1
  We were grave lovers. Love is past
XXX 5
  And sweet were the words she said to me.
XXXI 4

west
  Piercing the west,
Tutto 2

wet
  'Twas Irish humour, wet and dry,
Gas 19

what
  What counsel has the hooded moon
XII 1
  What sound hath made thy heart to fear?
XXVI 4
  Will choose her what you see to mouth upon.
A Memory 11
  I wish you could see what tears I weep
Gas 75

What-do-you-Colm
  I printed Patrick What-do-you-Colm:
Gas 44

when
  At that hour when all things have repose,
III 1
  When all things repose do you alone
III 6

At that hour when soft lights come and go,
III 13
When the shy star goes forth in heaven
IV 1
When he at eventide is calling,
IV 8
Love is unhappy when love is away!
IX 9
When thou hast heard his name upon
XI 7
When friends him fail.
XVIII 4
Unhappy when we draw apart
XXIII 3
When the heart is heaviest.
XXV 12
When over us the wild winds blow --
XXIX 10
When one at twilight shyly played
XXX 2
When the bat flew from tree to tree
XXXI 2
When the year takes them in the fall.
XXXIII 12
Sad as the sea-bird is, when going
XXXV 3
I moan in sleep when I hear afar their whirling laughter.
XXXVI 6
When the dear love she yielded with a sigh
Tutto 11
Raised when she has and shaken
Nightpiece 11
While they console him when he whinges
The Holy Office 27
Or him who once when snug abed
The Holy Office 43
At night when close in bed she lies
The Holy Office 69
When I think of the emigrant train and ship.
Gas 76

whenever
Whenever publicly we meet
The Holy Office 67

where
Strings by the river where
I 3

where (continued)

Where no rude wind might visit me.
VI 3

Where only peace might be my part.
VI 8

Where the gay winds do most desire
VII 3

There, where the gay winds stay to woo
VII 5

And where the sky's a pale blue cup
VII 9

Where softly-burning fires appear,
XV 6

Where Love did sometime go.
XVI 4

Where the great pine - forest
XX 7

That night allures me where alarms
XXII 9

Where soul with soul lies prisoned.
XXII 12

Neither a love where may not be
XXVII 11

The shadowy garden where love is.
XXIX 8

Come, my beloved, where I may
XXXII 7

Where Love did so sweet music make
XXXIII 2

Where I go.
XXXV 8

Where my dark lover lies.
She Weeps 2

In the still garden where a child
Simples 3

Where brooding day stares down upon the sea
Flood 7

Where they have crouched and crawled and prayed
The Holy Office 83

Firm as the mountain-ridges where
The Holy Office 87

Where Christ and Caesar are hand and glove!
Gas 26

O lovely land where the shamrock grows!
Gas 27

Where they talk of "bastard," "bugger" and "whore,"
Gas 32

wherefore
Wherefore receive now from my lip
The Holy Office 9

whereto
Whereto I pass at even of day,
Bahnhofstrasse 2

which
Which now is ended in this way.
XXXIII 6
Through which I lost my diadem,
The Holy Office 52
Those things for which Grandmother Church
The Holy Office 53

while
From furrow to furrow, while overhead
IX 3
While sweetly, gently, secretly,
XV 9
While they console him when he whinges
The Holy Office 27

whines
Wind whines and whines the shingle,
On the Beach 1

whinges
While they console him when he whinges
The Holy Office 27

whining
From whining wind and colder
On the Beach 5

whips
Disdaining the reins, with fluttering whips, the charioteers.
XXXVI 4

whirling
I moan in sleep when I hear afar their whirling laughter.
XXXVI 6

whisper
The sly reeds whisper to the night
Alone 5

whistling
The wind is whistling merrily.
XXXIII 10

white
White breast of the dove,
XIV 11
Frail the white rose and frail are
A Flower 1
My scarlet leaves them white as wool:
The Holy Office 57

who
One who is singing by your gate.
IV 4
Nor muse: Who may this singer be
IV 9
Who goes amid the green wood
VIII 1
Who goes amid the merry green wood
VIII 3
Who passes in the sunlight
VIII 5
Who passes in the sweet sunlight
VIII 7
Who was my friend.
XVII 8
So he who has sorrow
XVIII 15
He who hath glory lost, nor hath
XXI 1
Who a mad tale bequeaths to us
XXVI 9
Who gathers simples of the moon.
Simples 12
Him who is, him who was!
A Prayer 12
I, who dishevelled ways forsook
The Holy Office 3
Who safe at ingle-nook, by proxy,
The Holy Office 17
Like him who finds a joy at table
The Holy Office 19
With him who hies him to appease
The Holy Office 25
Or him who sober all the day
The Holy Office 29

Or him who plays the ragged patch
The Holy Office 33
Or him who will his hat unfix
The Holy Office 37
Or him who loves his Master dear --
The Holy Office 41
Or him who drinks his pint in fear --
The Holy Office 42
Or him who once when snug abed
The Holy Office 43
Who soars above on an angel's wing
Gas 46
Who was it said: Resist not evil?
Gas 85

whom
For whom does all the sunny woodland
VIII 11
But all these men of whom I speak
The Holy Office 47

whore
Where they talk of "bastard," "bugger" and "whore,"
Gas 32

whose
Whose way in heaven is aglow
III 12
Whose song about my heart is falling?
IV 10
Wind of spices whose song is ever
XIII 3
Whose leaves the morn admonisheth.
XV 4
Nor have I known a love whose praise
XXVII 9
Whose soul is sere and paler
A Flower 3
Grey way whose violet signals are
Bahnhofstrasse 3
Or him whose conduct "seems to own"
The Holy Office 31

why
Dear heart, why will you use me so?
XXIX 1
Alas! why will you use me so?
XXIX 12

why (continued)

My love, my love, my love, why have you left me alone?
XXXVI 12

Why then, remembering those shy
Tutto 9

To hear why earth and heaven trembled
Gas 2

I pity the poor -- that's why I took
Gas 65

That's why I publish far and wide
Gas 77

wide

Shy thoughts and grave wide eyes and hands
II 9

That's why I publish far and wide
Gas 77

wild

The wild bees hum.
X 12

When over us the wild winds blow --
XXIX 10

No more will the wild wind that passes
Watching 7

A wonder wild
A Flower 6

will

That will not after,
X 6

And soon will your true love be with you,
XIII 15

And there, love, will we go
XVI 2

And there, love, will we stay.
XVI 8

Will softly move
XVIII 10

The wrens will divers treasures keep,
XXIII 8

Dear heart, why will you use me so?
XXIX 1

Alas! why will you use me so?
XXIX 12

Yet will we kiss, sweetheart, before
XXXIII 15

My kiss will give peace now
XXXIV 9
No more will the wild wind that passes
Watching 7
Will choose her what you see to mouth upon.
A Memory 11
Blind me with your dark nearness, O have mercy, beloved enemy of my will!
A Prayer 7
Myself unto myself will give
The Holy Office 1
Or him who will his hat unfix
The Holy Office 37
This very next lent I will unbare
Gas 91
My awful sin I will confess.
Gas 94

Williams's
Downes's cakeshop and Williams's jam?
Gas 58

willow
The sun is in the willow leaves
XXIV 5

willows
The willows meet.
I 4

win
And tried so hard to win for us
The Holy Office 45

wind
Do you hear the night wind and the sighs
III 3
And the night wind answering in antiphon
III 9
Where no rude wind might visit me.
VI 3
Wind of spices whose song is ever
XIII 3
Now, wind, of your good courtesy
XIII 9
Singing: The bridal wind is blowing
XIII 13

wind (continued)
Along with us the summer wind
XXXI 5
The wind is whistling merrily.
XXXIII 10
No more will the wild wind that passes
Watching 7
Wind whines and whines the shingle,
On the Beach 1
From whining wind and colder
On the Beach 5

window
Lean out of the window,
V 1
V 16

And sing at her window;
XIII 12

winds
Where the gay winds do most desire
VII 3
There, where the gay winds stay to woo
VII 5
Winds of May, that dance on the sea,
IX 1
For the winds of May!
IX 8
The odorous winds are weaving
XIV 5
Desolate winds assail with cries
XXIX 7
When over us the wild winds blow --
XXIX 10
He hears the winds cry to the waters'
XXXV 5
The grey winds, the cold winds are blowing
XXXV 7

wing
Who soars above on an angel's wing
Gas 46

wings
Vast wings above the lambent waters brood
Flood 3

winter
The voice of the winter
XXXIV 5

O sleep, for the winter
XXXIV 7

He travels after a winter sun,
Tilly 1

wisdom
My heart, have you no wisdom thus to despair?
XXXVI 11

Nor old heart's wisdom yet to know
Bahnhofstrasse 7

wise
Believe me rather that am wise
XII 7

And the wise choirs of faery
XV 11

Shall we not be as wise as they
XXIII 11

Dearest, my lips wax all too wise;
XXVII 8

wish
I wish you could see what tears I weep
Gas 75

witchery
For I have heard of witchery
XXIV 11

within
Because within my hand I held
XVII 3

without
Saw Jesus Christ without his head
The Holy Office 44

For I detect without surprise
The Holy Office 63

Without the consent of Billy Walsh.
Gas 24

withstand
I dare not withstand the cold touch that I dread.
A Prayer 8

witty
The mind of witty Aristotle,
The Holy Office 6

woe
Though thy heart presage thee woe,
XXV 2

woman's
And some woman's legs that I can't recall,
Gas 34

wonder
A wonder wild
A Flower 6
It's a wonder to me, upon my soul,
Gas 61

woo
There, where the gay winds stay to woo
VII 5
Happy Love is come to woo
XI 3
Thee and woo thy girlish ways --
XI 4
And softly woo him
XVIII 11
Soft arms that woo me to relent
XXII 3
And woo me to detain.
XXII 4

wood
Who goes amid the green wood
VIII 1
Who goes amid the merry green wood
VIII 3

woodland
The ways of all the woodland
VIII 9
For whom does all the sunny woodland
VIII 11

woods
The woods their rich apparel wear --
VIII 14

wool
My scarlet leaves them white as wool:
The Holy Office 57

word
There is no word nor any sign
XVII 5
From far a low word breathes on the breaking brain
A Prayer 3
From far her low word breathe on my breaking brain.
A Prayer 15
I printed it all to the very last word
Gas 9
And a play on the Word and Holy Paul
Gas 33

worded
Love's breath in you is stale, worded or sung,
A Memory 5

words
Their words come to.
XVIII 8
And sweet were the words she said to me.
XXXI 4

works
The long-lost works of Aeschylus.
The Holy Office 46

world
The world that was not
Ecce Puer 11

would
I would in that sweet bosom be
VI 1
VI 5
I would be ever in that heart
VI 6
I would we lay,
XX 2
That answers my corruptive "would."
The Holy Office 66

wrap
Clouds that wrap the vales below
XXV 8

wrap (continued)
Grey sea I wrap him warm
On the Beach 6

wrath
Among his foes in scorn and wrath
XXI 3

wrens
The wrens will divers treasures keep,
XXIII 8

writer
Of an Irish writer in foreign parts.
Gas 4

writers
Her writers and artists to banishment
Gas 16

writer's
And I saw the writer's foul intent.
Gas 12

writing
And writing of Dublin, dirty and dear,
Gas 53

written
Written by Moore, a genuine gent
Gas 35

wrote
And a play he wrote (you've read it, I'm sure)
Gas 31

Wyse
To O'Leary Curtis and John Wyse Power
Gas 52

year
When the year takes them in the fall.
XXXIII 12
The year, the year is gathering.
XXXIII 18

years
He sent me a book ten years ago:
Gas 5

yellow
She bends upon the yellow keys,
II 7
The snood upon thy yellow hair.
XI 6
A rogue in red and yellow dress
XXXIII 7
That was over her dressed in Austrian yellow,
Gas 50

yes
My hope and all my riches -- yes! --
XXIII 5

yet
Yet must thou fold me unaware
XXVII 3
Yet will we kiss, sweetheart, before
XXXIII 15
Rosefrail and fair -- yet frailest
A Flower 5
Nor old heart's wisdom yet to know
Bahnhofstrasse 7

yield
Come, give, yield all your strength to me!
A Prayer 2
Come! I yield. Bend deeper upon me! I am here.
A Prayer 16

yielded
When the dear love she yielded with a sigh
Tutto 11

you
Do you hear the night wind and the sighs
III 3
When all things repose do you alone
III 6
Hear you amid the drowsy even
IV 3
And he is come to visit you.
IV 6
Know you by this, the lover's chant,
IV 11
I heard you singing
V 3
For I heard you singing
V 11
Saw you my true love anywhere?
IX 6

you (continued)

All you that love.
X 4

I pray you go,
XIII 10

And soon will your true love be with you,
XIII 15

And hear you not the thrushes calling,
XVI 5

O Sweetheart, hear you
XVIII 1

Prefer a lying clamour before you:
XIX 2

Can they dishonour you?
XIX 4

I pray you, cease to comb out,
XXIV 9

Dear heart, why will you use me so?
XXIX 1

Still are you beautiful -- but O,
XXIX 3

But you, dear love, too dear to me,
XXIX 11

Alas! why will you use me so?
XXIX 12

O you unquiet heart!
XXXIV 2
XXXIV 12

My heart, have you no wisdom thus to despair?
XXXVI 11

My love, my love, my love, why have you left me alone?
XXXVI 12

Love's breath in you is stale, worded or sung,
A Memory 5

Will choose her what you see to mouth upon.
A Memory 11

Ladies and gents, you are here assembled
Gas 1

To show you for strictures I don't care a button
Gas 29

'Twould give you a heartburn on your arse:
Gas 40

Shite and onions! Do you think I'll print
Gas 55

Colm can tell you I made a rebate
Gas 71

I wish you could see what tears I weep
Gas 75

young
The young leaves as they pass,
VII 6
That is so young and fair.
VIII 16
I heard their young hearts crying
Watching 1
The clear young eyes' soft look, the candid brow,
Tutto 5
And moonlight kisses her young brow
Simples 6
Young life is breathed
Ecce Puer 9

your
One who is singing by your gate.
IV 4
'Tis I that am your visitant.
IV 12
Now, wind, of your good courtesy
XIII 9
And soon will your true love be with you,
XIII 15
My breast shall be your bed.
XIV 12
Because your voice was at my side
XVII 1
Your hand again.
XVII 4
Your lover's tale;
XVIII 2
Comb out your long hair,
XXIV 10
How is your beauty raimented!
XXIX 4
Through the clear mirror of your eyes,
XXIX 5
Speak to your heart.
XXXII 8
And quiet to your heart --
XXXIV 10
Vainly your loveblown bannerets mourn!
Watching 6
Your clustered fruits to love's full flood,
Flood 10
Your lean jaws grin with. Lash
A Memory 3

your (continued)

Your itch and quailing, nude greed of the flesh.
A Memory 4

Pluck forth your heart, saltblood, a fruit of tears.
A Memory 13

Come, give, yield all your strength to me!
A Prayer 2

Blind me with your dark nearness, O have mercy, beloved enemy of my will!
A Prayer 7

Forgive your son!
Ecce Puer 16

Though (asking your pardon) as for the verse
Gas 39

'Twould give you a heartburn on your arse:
Gas 40

youth

Highhearted youth comes not again
Bahnhofstrasse 6

you've

And a play he wrote (you've read it, I'm sure)
Gas 31

zone

The zone that doth become thee fair,
XI 5